May 2017

Ron Auch Sr.
1107 27th Ave,
Kenosha, WI 53140

ISBN-13:
978-1546902195

ISBN-10:
1546902198

Cover by Megan Pennock

Table of Contents

Pray That You Might Escape

Introduction

This book will present a theory about the rapture of the Church, which will explain why there are so many different opinions about when the rapture will take place. Let us be clear at the outset; different opinions about the rapture have nothing to do with a man's salvation. We are still brothers and sisters in Christ no matter what position we hold to. Subsequently, even though differing views exist, it doesn't make a lot of difference in the end. Someone very wisely once said that when the seventh seal is opened in Revelation chapter eight, and there is thirty minutes of silence in Heaven, that's when God gives all the prophecy teachers a chance to correct their end-time flow charts.

Some say that the whole body of Christ will be raptured before the Great Tribulation; this is the Pre-Tribulation theory. Others believe that the whole body of the saved must go through the first half of the Great Tribulation before they are raptured; which is the Mid-Tribulation theory. Some believe that all Christians living at the time, will go through the entire tribuation period and be raptured at the very end of it, which, of course is the Post-Tribulation position.

Yet there is another position. Along with the three most poplular positions of, Pre-trib, Mid-trib and Post-trib there are those who believe in the Partial Rapture theory. The Partial Rapture theory holds to the idea that the rapture is only for the overcoming Christians.

Well-known believers are found in each of these schools of thought. Those in the Pre-trib camp include J. N. Darby, William Kelly (C. H. Spurgeon once said that Kelly's brain was as large as the universe), Phillips Brooks, C. I. Scofield, and so forth. Those in the Mid-trib position are men like Gleason L. Archer, Richard Reiter, Norman B. Harrison, James Oliver Buswell, and Marvin Rosenthal. Those in the Post-trib school include such names as George Muller, A. J. Gordon, A. B. Simpson, W. J. Erdman, W. G. Moorehead, Henry Frost of Canada, and James Wright.

The Partial Rapture theory has such names as Hudson Taylor, Robert Chapman, Robert Govett (Spurgeon praised his writings as having light a century ahead of his time and as being full of gold), G. H. Pember, D. M. Panton (the "prince of prophecy"), Watchman Nee, and others.

Though this book leans toward the Partial Rapture theory, that is not our only intent. The author of this book believes the classical Partial Rapture theory has a lot of merit, but at the same time, it presents some major theological problems.

The purpose of this book is not to settle any and all questions about when the rapture of the Church is going to take place. It's intent is to cause the reader to determine whether or not they are ready for the rapture regardless of when it happens. The author's opinion on this subject is that the Pre-trib rapture is the best position to hold on this subject, but that it falls somewhat short of all God wants us to see and understand concerning this great event.

So now we have our first dilemma. How can everybody's different positions on this subject be correct and provable through the scriptures? The answer is simple. They each have a certain degree of correctness. We will gain a greater revelation of this great event through a blending of each view, with one view being the dominant one. We believe that to be the Pre-trib perspective. Our larger intention is for the reader to come away with a greater desire to live in a way that pleases God, so as to be ready when He comes for us.

Part One
Who goes, who stays?

Chapter One

The Rapture's Purpose

The primary purpose for the rapture of the Church is not just so that the Church can avoid some pending judgment on earth. It's much deeper than that.

Many people believe that if you are a saved person you will automatically go in the rapture. They believe the rapture is inclusive with salvation. This is a huge issue. Changing our thinking on this issue is critical. A careful examination of the scriptures will reveal that it does not teach that anywhere. There are far more indications that not all will go in the rapture of the Church than all going. In fact there are no scriptural references of everyone going all at once. We only have conjecture on that.

In Luke 21 Jesus is asked a question about the end times:

Luke 21:7 "Teacher," they asked, "when will these things happen? And what will be the sign that they are about to take place?"

Jesus then goes into a discussion about the Tribulation period and all the tragedy that will come to the earth. Then he ends his comments with this:

Luke 21:36 "**Be always on the watch, and <u>pray</u> <u>that you may be able to escape</u> all that is about to happen, and that you may be able to stand before the Son of Man."**

Jesus is talking to his disciples in these verses. If the rapture of the Church automatically includes everyone who is born again, why does Jesus tell his disciples to be on the watch and to pray that they may be able to escape all that is about to happen?

Let's look at a couple of Greek meanings here. First he says to watch. 'Watch' is the Greek word agrupneo (ag-roop-neh'-o); it means to be sleepless, i.e. keep awake.

Does Jesus mean this literally? Are we not supposed to sleep? Is he saying that if we sleep at night He might come and we would miss the rapture? Nobody believes that. We all have to sleep. It is not unSpiritual to sleep physically. Jesus slept. However, it is a dangerous thing to sleep Spiritually. Answer me this; can you fall asleep Spiritually, if you have never awakened Spiritually? That would be impossible; therefore, we must conclude that this warning goes out to those who are awake and who face the possibility of falling asleep and subsequently going through all the difficulties Jesus described.

This is a warning to the Church. The non-Christian is already asleep Spiritually – in fact, they have never been awakened yet. Why would Jesus say to someone who is sleeping, "make sure you don't fall asleep?" He would only say that to those who are currently awake.

Then there is the phrase "that you may be able." Katischuo (kat-is-khoo'-o); to overpower: prevail (against). This speaks of a Spiritual strength we all need to be able to prevail against the Spirit of the day.

In Revelation 2 we read more about the overcomer:

Revelation 2:7 "To him who overcomes, I will give the right to eat from the tree of life."

If we break down this verse a little, we find: Greek - Overcome - nikao (nik-ah'-o); to subdue (literally or figuratively): conquer, overcome, prevail, get the victory.

My paraphrase of this verse would be: Be always on the watch, (don't fall asleep) and pray that you may be able (pray that you will have the power) to escape all that is about to happen,

If this warning is going out to the Church, why is it? If going in the rapture was automatically included with salvation, there would be no need for a warning. It would be illogical to warn us of something that is automatically going to take place. The Bible does not teach that going in the rapture is inclusive with salvation. That is what we have to eradicate from our thinking because there is no biblical basis for it. There is no guarantee anywhere that says the rapture is automatic with salvation. Salvation addresses the issue of sin in a person's life. The rapture of the Church is a separate event entirely. Since so many believe that the rapture is inclusive with salvation, we have developed many different perspectives as to when it will take place, whether, Pre, Mid, or Post, Tribulation. We are going to build off of this premise - only the overcoming Christian will go in the rapture regardless of whether that's the Pre-trib, Mid-trib, or Post-trib rapture.

When we speak of the rapture of the Church, we are referring to the catching up of the saints to meet the Lord in the air.

1 Thessalonians 4:16-17 "For the Lord himself will come down from heaven, with a loud command, with the voice of the archangel and with the trumpet call of God, and the dead in Christ will rise first. (17) After that, we who are still alive and are left will be caught up together with them in the clouds to meet the Lord in the air. And so we will be with the Lord forever."

The rapture of the Church is often called the coming of the Lord, but never, the second coming of the Lord. The rapture must never be referred to as the second coming because He does not come to earth at that time. At the rapture Christ does not appear visibly to those on the earth, but He comes in the air above the earth to "catch up" or

11

"rapture" the dead and living saints who rise together to meet the Lord in the air. Notice in 1 Thessalonians 4:17, it uses the phrase "caught up." The Bible does not use the word "rapture." We have merely adapted that word since it means the same thing.

These two comings cannot be mixed, if the doctrine is to be clear. The scriptures that apply to the rapture do not apply to the Second Coming. This is where a lot of confusion about when the rapture is going to take place comes in. Matthew 24 is often referred to as a proof text that the rapture of the Church is not until the end of the Tribulation.

Matthew 24:6-9 "You will hear of wars and rumors of wars, but see to it that you are not alarmed. Such things must happen, but the end is still to come. (7) Nation will rise against nation, and kingdom against kingdom. There will be famines and earthquakes in various places. (8) All these are the beginning of birth pains. (9) "Then you will be handed over to be persecuted and put to death, and you will be hated by all nations because of me."

This sounds very much like there will be Christians in the Tribulation and that they will be persecuted even unto death. However, if we go to verse 15 of the same chapter we get a clearer picture of what is going on.

Matthew 24:15 "So when you see standing in the holy place 'the abomination that causes desolation,' spoken of through the prophet Daniel-let the reader understand-

The abomination of desolation is when the antichrist declares himself to be God. This takes place in the middle of the Tribulation period. The next few verses go on to describe the great Tribulation on earth.

Matthew 24:30-31 "At that time the sign of the Son of Man will appear in the sky, and all the nations of the earth will mourn. They will see the Son of Man coming on the clouds of the sky, with power and great glory. (31) And he will send his angels with a loud trumpet call, and they will gather his elect from the four winds, from one end of the heavens to the other."

This is a reference that the Post-trib people use to justify their position stating that Jesus gathers all his elect to heaven with him, just prior to his Second coming. However, this message was written to the Jews that are living during the Tribulation. This was not written to the Church. As we continue to read we will see this.

Matthew 24:32-33 "Now learn this lesson from the fig tree: As soon as its twigs get tender and its leaves come out, you know that summer is near. (33) Even so, when you see all these things, you know that it is near, right at the door.

The fig tree has always been a reference to Israel. The verse could be paraphrased to say, *"Learn this lesson about Israel.*" Israel has rejected her savior. Subsequently, at the Pre-trib rapture, very few Jews will go. Only those who are born again today will go, if they are living an overcoming life.

At the "abomination of desolation" when the antichrist declares himself as God, the Spiritual blindness will come off the eyes of Israel and they will realize they have been deceived. They are then told to flee to the mountains to escape the Tribulation that will come on the earth. Those who see that the antichrist is not the true Messiah are what the Bible calls "the elect." Once they realize that the antichrist is a false god they will then turn to the true Messiah and, subsequently, die as martyrs during the Tribulation. God then gathers the elect at the end of the Tribulation. So there is a Post-trib rapture, a Mid-trib rapture and a Pre-trib rapture.

After the Second Coming, (when Jesus comes back to earth), is the time called the Millennium. The Millennium is the thousand-year reign of Christ on earth. Actually the rapture is secondary in nature compared to the issue of the overcoming Christian ruling and reigning with Christ, as Revelation chapter 20 and verse 6 indicates.

Revelation 20:6 "Blessed and holy are those who have part in the first resurrection. The second death has no power over them, but they will be priests of God and of Christ and will reign with him for a thousand years."

The Overcomers

Matthew 25 begins with the parable of the Ten Virgins. We will deal in much more detail about this parable in a following chapter. However, this parable is a very clear teaching that not everyone who possessed the lamp of salvation will go in the rapture – only the wise go. After the parable of the Ten Virgins Jesus then teaches another parable, the parable of the talents, about how God has left each of us with talents that are to be used in the kingdom.

Look at what he says to those who used their talents wisely.

Matthew 25:21 "His lord said unto him, Well done, thou good and faithful servant: thou hast been faithful over a few things, I will make thee ruler over many things: enter thou into the joy of thy lord." KVJ

Being made a ruler of many things is a reference to ruling and reigning with Christ during the Millennium. This is what all of this comes down to. We gain salvation by accepting Christ into our lives. If you have the Son of God living in you, you do indeed have eternal life, and you will have eternal life even if you miss the rapture. Missing the rapture does not equal being Spiritually lost. The idea of the imminent return of Christ, or the rapture, is to be a motivator for us to live our lives fully for Christ so that we can reign with Him in the Millennium. And if we do not live fully for Christ, we will not reign with Him. However, not reigning with Christ is not equal to being lost.

Revelation 20:4-6 "I saw thrones on which were seated those who had been given authority to judge. And I saw the souls of those who had been beheaded because of their testimony for Jesus and because of the word of God. They had not worshiped the beast or his image and had not received his mark on their foreheads or their hands. They came to life and reigned with Christ a thousand years. (5) (The rest of the dead did not come to life until the thousand years were ended.) This is the first resurrection. (6) Blessed and holy are those who have part in the first resurrection. The second death has no power over them, but they will be priests of God and of Christ and will reign with him for a thousand years."

These verses are used by those who hold to the Post-trib position claiming that these verses refer to Christians who went through the Great Tribulation and died as martyrs. Suddenly, these multitudes show up in heaven. They came to life (after being beheaded) and reigned with Christ a thousand years. These verses are also used by Pre-tribers as a proof text that there was a great revival during the Tribulation period. Since they believe that all Christians were raptured in the beginning of the Tribulation, it makes sense to them that many people came into faith during the Tribulation.

There is not one reference of a great revival happening during the Tribulation. It is merely assumed. The messages to the seven Churches of Asia are in Revelation chapters 2 and 3. In chapter 4 we have what many believe to be a Pre-trib rapture in verse 1.

Rev. 4:1 "After this I looked, and there before me was a door standing open in heaven. And the voice I had first heard speaking to me like a trumpet said, "Come up here, and I will show you what must take place after this..."

This is typically considered a reference to the rapture when John is called to heaven. This is also considered the end of the Church age. The overcoming Church is called up to heaven at the rapture. Then we move into a different dispensation or age.

The Church stands distinct from Israel and did not begin until the Day of Pentecost: thus it did not exist in the Old Testament period. According to this view, the distinction is so pronounced between Israel and the Church, that Israel is seen as existing in a 'time out' period while God is busy with the Church. Once the Church Age ends, at the rapture, God's plan for Israel resumes.

After John was called up to heaven, (Rev. 4:1), the word *repent* is used four times in the book of Revelation and in every case it says they repented *not*. The one possibility or exception are the Jews who turn to the Savior after the abomination of desolation. Consider these verses:

Revelation 9:20 "The rest of mankind who were not killed by these plagues still <u>did not repent</u> of the work of their hands; they did not stop worshiping demons, and idols of gold,"

Revelation 9:21 "<u>Nor did they repent</u> of their murders, their magic arts, their sexual immorality or their thefts."

Revelation 16:9 "They were seared by the intense heat and they cursed the name of God, who had control over these plagues, but <u>they refused to repent</u> and glorify him."

Revelation 16:11 "and cursed the God of heaven because of their pains and their sores, but <u>they refused to repent</u> of what they had done."

Even in the midst of the worst plagues there was no repentance. There is no biblical evidence of a world-wide revival during the Tribulation period.

What we begin to see is that the rapture of the Church is for the overcoming Christian. The purpose of the rapture is to determine who will rule and reign with Christ during the mileniumm. It does not make a lot of practical sense to believe that everyone who has ever named the name of Christ qualifies as an overcoming Christian? The non-overcoming Christian - Paul refers to as carnal-Christians - will not go in the rapture. Subsequently, they will go through the Tribulation and gain their overcoming status by dying as martyrs, and ruling with Christ for His thousand year reign.

The Bible actually teaches that many who name the name of Christ will be left to go through the Tribulation because they chose not to prepare themselves to rule and reign with Christ by living as an overcomer. Here is where this can be a bit confusing. For too long we have been taught, without any biblical precedent, that if you miss the rapture it's because you are not a Christian. That is not true at all: missing the rapture means you failed to live an overcoming life and, subsequently, will be left on earth to gain the status of overcomer by dying as a martyr.

Let's examine this issue further. Why would someone be left behind? Why would Christ leave someone behind who has given his or her life to Him? The simple answer to that is, according to scripture, they lived foolishly and carnally, as the parable of the ten virgins teaches. The attraction to this world became more important to them than God's kingdom. They were not overcomers, and it's the overcomers who reign with Christ during the Millennium.

The Holy Spirit

2 Thessalonians 2:6-7 "And now you know what is holding him back, so that he may be revealed at the proper time. (7) For the secret power of lawlessness is already at work; but the one who now holds it back will continue to do so till he is taken out of the way."

Many scholars agree that the restraining power that is keeping the antichrist from coming into full power is the Holy Spirit. At the time of the Pre-trib rapture the overcoming Christians are removed from the earth. They are the only ones who have any restraining power. They have overcome the world, subsequently, becoming that which restrains evil. Do carnal Christians sway society? Do carnal Christians, those who are living for this world, have any restraining influence? Can a carnal Church impact society?

These verses in 2 Thessalonians do not imply that Jesus mysteriously removes the Holy Spirit from this world. He's not going to remove His Spirit from those who posess it. The scripture states; **"God will never leave us nor forsake us."** The carnal Christians who miss the rapture will continue to posses what they currently have. However, the carnal Christian has no restraining power because he lives for the world. How could anyone who lives for the world influence it towards godliness?

If God removes the only group of people who influence men towards godliness, how will men get saved after that? No man comes to the Father unless the one who sent him draws him. The Holy Spirit draws men. Without His influence there will be no drawing, hence no revival during the Tribulation.

Consider this: carnal Christians have a difficult time living for God right now while the Holy Spirit has full influence. What makes us think, that if some Christians have a hard time living for Him today that once the influence of the Holy Spirit is removed there is going to be a great revival among those who have been rejecting his influence all their lives? What the scripture indicates is that a large group of people calling themselves Christians today, who do not live for him, will suddenly, Spiritually, wake up after the rapture of the Church and then prove their faith by dying as a martyr.

The Church is full of nominal Christians who refuse to live holy and pure. I believe they are saved because we are saved by grace. I do not believe that they will go in the Pre-trib rapture of the Church.

Popular theology dictates that most of those who do not go in the rapture are what we called backsliders. We call them that because they are obviously not living for the Lord and yet at one point in their life they submitted their life to

Christ. However, if you talk heart to heart with most people who once lived for God, but today would be categorized as backslidden, you'll find that most of them still profess a love for God; they still talk kindly about the kingdom. I wonder if the term carnal Christian would apply better here.

The Rest of the Dead

In Revelation 20:5, we read: **"(The rest of the dead did not come to life until the thousand years were ended.) This is the first resurrection."** This refers to those who did not come to life until the thousand years were over. Who are these people? If they come to life after the Millennium, which makes them a part of the first resurrection, who are they, and why are the not part of the Millennial Reign?

Revelation 20:6 "Blessed and holy are those who have part in the first resurrection. The second death has no power over them, but they will be priests of God and of Christ and will reign with him for a thousand years."

The rest of the dead, who did not come back to life until the thousand years were ended, seem to be the Christians who died in a carnal state. Is it reasonable to think that some scoundrel, who fought God all his life, never did a thing to advance the Kingdom of God, and gets saved on his deathbed just weeks before he dies, is now going to reign and rule with Christ as an overcoming Christian? No they are not

– they don't come back to life until the thousand years are finished. When they die they go to heaven and stay there throughout the millenial reign of Christ.

They are indeed saved because we are saved by grace, but they did not gain the status of overcomer. This is why I stated earlier that, if a person misses the rapture it does not mean they are not Christian, it merely means they chose to live carnally and must pay a price for their decision (a full description of a 'carnal Christian' is, is found in chapter 3).

Barnes Notes: *To say that they "lived not" during that period is only in comparison to the eminent saints and martyrs who reign with Christ. Because these people are saved they are in the presence of God. However, they do not come into remembrance; their principles were not what then characterized the Church.*

The primary idea behind this book is that we either learn how to overcome the attractions of this world or they will overcome us. If we live a carnal existence we will not be able to rule and reign with Christ during the Millennium. I want to clarify once again that the carnal Christian is indeed saved. To not make it in the first rapture does not mean they were not saved. It means they lived foolishly; they did not attempt to do anything for the Lord; the world was far more attractive to them than Spiritual disciplines, and so forth.

Ruling and reigning is limited to those who lived an overcoming life.

So the question must be asked, *"Where are the rest of the dead during the thousand years?"* I believe they are in heaven. They are in the same place anyone of us would be if we were to die as believers today. It is an existence that is separate from this world. To be absent from the body is to be present with the Lord. Both the overcomer and those who were overcome go to heaven when they die. Heaven is not our eternal home. Heaven is only going to exist until the thousand year reign of Christ is over. After that, this old earth gets a face-lift and this world becomes our eternal home.

If you die as a carnal Christian, you will not reign with Christ during the Millennium, but you will ultimately live eternally with Him. Salvation is by the blood of Christ. Ruling and reigning is determined by the works we do today.

The Parable of the Talents

Matthew 25:21 "His lord said unto him, Well done, thou good and faithful servant: thou hast been faithful over a few things, I will make thee ruler over many things: enter thou into the joy of thy lord." KVJ

In this parable a man was going on a journey so he entrusts his wealth to his servants, hoping they will invest it wisely and make a profit for him. The first two men did just that. When the man returned, they showed him the profit they made for him. To both of them he says, *"Enter into the joy of the Lord."* However, the third man did not make a profit for him, and because of that, he is cast into darkness where there is weeping and gnashing of teeth.

What is the purpose of this parable? If we think it teaches that a person must use their gifts in order to be saved that would go completely against grace and yet it seems that the man who did nothing lost out with the Master. So what is its purpose? What is the purpose of a parable that emphasizes the need to use our gifts for the Lord, if it's not teaching salvation by works?

The final words of the parable, *"I will make thee ruler over many things,"* tells us that this parable is meant to prepare us to reign with Christ by living an overcoming life here on earth and making the most of what God has given us. And those who do not live in a way that benefits the master go through a terrible time of weeping and gnashing of teeth. The weeping and gnashing of teeth refers to the time of Tribulation on earth. It cannot represent hell or that would be equal to saying that talents get you into heaven and if you don't use your talents you cannot be saved. This parable is all about ruling and reigning with Christ. It's a challenge to make the most of the life Jesus has given us so that we can enter into the joy of serving him in the millennium.

All three of the servants could be categorized the same. They were servants of their master. Two of them entered into the joy of the Lord, one did not because he did not live an overcoming life. Outside of this one thing (rulership), the parable of the talents would have no purpose.

All of the promises in the book of Revelation go to the overcomer.

Revelation 2:11 "He who overcomes will not be hurt at all by the second death."

The one who proves himself faithful over a few things will be made a ruler over many things. Proving ourselves faithful over a few things is a reference to the life we are living today. Those who prove themselves faithful are the overcomers.

Chapter Two

Judgement Seat of Christ

All Christians will experience the Judgement Seat of Christ. It will take place before Christ's second coming, in heaven. Its purpose is to establish the overcomer's rule in the millennial kingdom. Keep in mind that it takes place in heaven, which means whoever is a part of this event has made it to heaven. There is no need to fear this judgment as far as salvation is concerned. This is a judgment of our works only.

2 "Corinthians 5:10 For we must all appear before the Judgement Seat of Christ, so that each of us may receive what is due us for the things done while in the body, whether good or bad."

The Greek word for judgment is 'bema' and it means, a step. This is also referred to as the Bema Seat of Christ. The Bema Seat is a raised place mounted by steps. This could look very threatening to say the least. The idea of walking up some steps to stand before Jesus Christ and be judged is quite intimidating. However, the good thing about this is that it is for believers only. This is not a judgment of the believer's sins because they have been washed clean by the Savior's blood and God remembers them no more. This judgment is for the works each believer accomplished for God while on the earth, to find out whether they are good or bad works.

The Greek word for 'good' in this verse is *agathos* and is referenced as gold, silver, and costly stones. This is the work done by the believer who is walking in fellowship with the Lord and is controlled by the Holy Spirit - overcomer.

The Greek word for 'bad' in this verse is *phaulos* and refers to that which is worthless in the sight of God; thus it is referenced as wood, hay, and stubble. These will all be burned up by fire, thus a loss of rewards. These kinds of works would typify the carnal Christian. We can see by this that there will either be rewards or loss of rewards at this time. The rewards will be given for the believer's faithfulness to the Lord.

1 Corinthians 3:12-15 "If anyone builds on this foundation using gold, silver, costly stones, wood, hay or straw, (13) their work will be shown for what it is, because the Day will bring it to light. It will be revealed with fire, and the fire will test the quality of each person's work. (14) If what has been built survives, the builder will receive a reward. (15) If it is burned up, the builder will suffer loss but yet will be saved—even though only as one escaping through the flames."

If a man's work burns up, if what he did on earth did very little to glorify Christ, if his works were made of wood, hay, or stubble, it is going to burn up. He will receive no rewards, but he himself will be saved. Even the carnal Christian has the hope of eternity, but he will not reign with Christ because he did not live as an overcomer.

It is quite necessary that the service of every child of God be definitely scrutinized and evaluated. The Judgement Seat of Christ is necessary for the appointment of places of rulership and authority with Christ in His role as 'King of Kings and Lord of Lords,' at His revelation in power and glory. Christ's rewards are meant to provide a powerful incentive for an obedient life. In light of all of this, there is little wonder that the apostle Paul rigorously disciplined himself so that he would not be disqualified from the reward of reigning with Christ.

1 Corinthians 9:25-27 "Everyone who competes in the games goes into strict training. They do it to get a crown that will not last, but we do it to get a crown that will last forever. (26) Therefore I do not run like someone running aimlessly; I do not fight like a boxer beating the air. (27) No, I strike a blow to my body and make it my slave so that after I have preached to others, I myself will not be disqualified for the prize."

Paul's concern about being disqualified is a reference to ruling with Christ. Paul was not worried about losing his salvation; he was disciplining himself to make sure he lived an overcoming life. The Greek word, 'disqualified' in verse 27 is *adokimos,* meaning castaway, which is taken from the term, bad metals. It's referring to something that cannot bear the test applied to it. Paul is referring to the Judgement Seat of Christ and how all of his works will pass through the fire, which is why he makes his body a slave to himself so that he will not be disqualified for the prize of ruling and reigning with Jesus.

The Judgement Seat of Christ can be a time of great regret, or it can be an occasion of supreme joy. The rewards at the Judgement Seat of Christ are meant to provide a powerful incentive for an obedient life today.

Once a person grasps the idea of earning a place of rulership in the Millennium, their whole purpose for living an obedient life on earth today will move from a legalistic perspective to a grace perspective. Some might say, *Didn't you just state that we have to earn a place of rulership? Isn't that legalism?"* Not at all, legalism is an attempt to earn salvation and we are not talking about that. We are saved by grace; we are talking about earning a place of rulership.

We are focusing on the rapture of the Church, but in reality the Rapture itself is a very quick event. In the twinkling of an eye it's over. This is more about the Judgement Seat of Christ than anything else.

2 Corinthians 5:9-10 "So we make it our goal to please him, whether we are at home in the body or away from it. (10) For we must all appear before the Judgement Seat of Christ, that each one may receive what is due him for the things done while in the body, whether good or bad."

The Judgement Seat of Christ is the burning heart of this entire revelation. The carnal Christian will remain on earth at the time of the rapture, but if he chooses, he can gain the position of overcomer through martyrdom. We must all pay a price in order to rule and reign with Christ. The overcomer is willing to pay the price during this life. He has Spiritual pursuits and objectives. His life's goal is to glorify and beautify the Bride of Christ. The carnal Christian chooses not to pay the price today, and cannot be convinced of the importance of Spiritual pursuits and will, subsequently, pay the price during the Tribulation, if he wants to rule with Christ.

The word "goal" means to love and seek for honor. The verse could start off saying, So we love and seek for honor, to please him. This is the only legitimate ambition in the world. There is nothing else our lives should be given to than this one thing – to please Him. If we were taken up with this one ambition, don't you think all the other issues regarding the rapture of the Church would just take care of themselves?

1 Corinthians 5:10 starts off by saying, **"For we must**," - this is expressing a necessity inherent with divine justice. We must stand before Him; this is for the vindication of God's holiness. For we must all - all the apostles, all the prophets, all the martyrs, all the overcomers, even all the carnal Christians - eventually appear before Christ. The word "appear" means to be made manifest. Our works must be made manifest to our own consciences, to all the world, and above all else to the Judge. Everything that has transpired within us must be tested by the fire.

It all comes down to this: salvation is by grace; ruling with Christ is by works. That is what the Bema Seat is all about. We either have to accept this theory or we have to say that all the admonitions to live an obedient life are because salvation is earned by being good. If salvation is by grace alone (and it is), then why are we constantly warned about living in obedience to Christ? Why does Jesus give many warnings to the Church to get ready for His return? What is there to get ready if the rapture is inclusive with salvation? These verses are challenging us to get ready for the rapture – to live a life worthy of ruling with Christ one day.

My grandfather on my mom's side got saved on his death bed. Just weeks before he died a minister visited him and led him to the Lord. I loved my grandfather but my most vivid memories of him are of him sitting in the pool hall in Utica, South Dakota, a cigar hanging out of his mouth with smoke wafting upward, a bottle of whiskey by his side, while playing cards with his friends. He was a wonderful man but he was not a godly man by any means, yet he got saved just weeks before he died. When his works pass through the fire, I image most of them are going to burn up – but he himself will be saved (1Cor 3:15). He barely escaped the flames of hell.

However, because his works will burn up, he will not be given a place of rulership during the millennium. I believe He will be part of the rest of the dead who did not come to life (on earth) until the thousand years were ended.

Chapter Three

No Works, No Rapture, Still Saved

A subtitle for this chapter could be, No works, No rapture, Still saved. Disassociating the rapture with salvation is a very difficult concept to get into our thinking. We have heard for so many years that all Christians go in the rapture that it is difficult to see what the Bible actually teaches about the issue. We must understand that the rapture has nothing to do with salvation. The rapture is purely for the purpose of judging our works for placement of ruler-ship during the Millennial reign of Christ.

D. M. Panton (the "prince of prophecy" 1870-1955), the Founder and Proprietor, as well as Editor of Dawn, believed that God gave Dawn into his hands as an instrument for making known and maintaining doctrines, which though clearly enunciated in the Word of God, had become all but a dead letter to the majority of Christians. One of those doctrines was that of the Partial Rapture of the Church.

In Panton's book "The Judgement Seat of Christ," he states over and over that not everyone who names the name of Christ will go in the rapture of the Church, but that they indeed are saved if they have made Christ their savior.

Dr. A.T. Pierson once said, *"We enter our salvation by faith, our works determine our relative rank, place, and reward."* The whole idea of the Judgement Seat of Christ is that God rewards works. But works have nothing to do with how we get saved. Missing the rapture has nothing to do with whether or not a person is saved. It has to do with the kind of life they lived as a Christian. Some time ago John Calvin said, *"There is no inconsistency in saying that God rewards good works, provided we understand that, nevertheless, men obtain eternal life gratuitously."*

D.M. Panton also said, *"Even a casual study of the Word of God reveals that eternal life comes by faith, and that rewards for our works come after faith."* A pure life relates to works, not so much salvation. Scriptures relate saved souls to someone running a race; an athlete wrestling; a warrior fighting; a farmer sowing; a mason building, and then it states that God is a rewarder of those who diligently seek Him.

Hebrews 11:6 "And without faith it is impossible to please God, because anyone who comes to him must believe that he exists and that he rewards those who earnestly seek him."

There has always been a division in the Church between grace and works. Since it's true that we are saved by grace, we have shied away from works, and yet the Bible is full of examples of our need to do good works.

Ephesians 2:8-10 "For it is by grace you have been saved, through faith-and this not from yourselves, it is the gift of God- (9) not by works, so that no one can boast. (10) For we are God's workmanship, created in Christ Jesus to do good works, which God prepared in advance for us to do."

Ephesians 2:9 tells us that we cannot be saved by works; the following verse says we were created to do good works. However, there is no contradiction here. Ephesians 2:8-9 basically tell us that we are saved by grace and verse 10 tells us that works must follow our salvation, and that we are rewarded for our works. Keep this in mind. The rapture is one of the rewards for our works. No works, no rapture, still saved.

Many Churches preach what could at best be called a legalistic, or a "works" gospel. We evangelicals preach grace. Dr. A.J. Gordon said, *"Just as a legalist resents the doctrine that good works can have no part in effecting our forgiveness, we evangelicals recoil from the idea that they can constitute any grounds for our reward."* There need not be this confusion because the two really have no relationship to one another. Grace and works really have no effect on each other. Grace is for salvation, works are for rewards and ruler-ship.

Luke 6:35 "But love your enemies, do good to them, and lend to them without expecting to get anything back. Then your reward will be great."

When we examine the Word of God we see first of all that God rewards god likeness, and god like conduct. Love your enemies; do good to them; lend to them freely, then your reward will be great. Is this talking about the reward of salvation? It couldn't be. That would be a gospel of works, and, if we can earn our way into heaven, then the Son of God did not need to come and die for us. Yet there is a reward for good works.

Matthew 6:6 "But when you pray, go into your room, close the door and pray to your Father, who is unseen. Then your Father, who sees what is done in secret, will reward you."

Not only will the prayer be answered because you prayed, but the praying itself will be rewarded. The act of praying is one of the good works that we can be storing up in heaven. Later in this same chapter Jesus tells us that these types of activities are what is called, storing up treasures in heaven.

Matthew 6:20-21 "But store up for yourselves treasures in heaven, where moth and rust do not destroy, and where thieves do not break in and steal. (21) For where your treasure is, there your heart will be also."

Every prayer we pray; every act of kindness and mercy we perform; every time we choose purity over profanity; and every attitude coming from us which emulates the Son of God, is being recorded and stored in heaven. And at the Judgement Seat of Christ those types of works will pass through the fire and come out the other side as precious stone, silver and gold.

Secure

Since we are saying that only the overcoming Christian will go in the rapture and the nominal Christian or the carnal Christian will not go in the rapture, it will be important to clarify our theology here. Many Arminianist use the term "backslidden" a little too loosely. It might be more proper to refer to those who once knew the Lord but are not actively serving him as carnal Christians rather than backslidden. To backslide is very serious. To be a carnal Christian is quite common.

I once heard Dr. Gordon Anderson, former President of North Central University in Minneapolis, MN., teach on this issue in a most excellent way. He told us to create an imaginary line with an imaginary man trying to get from under the line to the top side of the line. The line represents the division between being saved and not saved. Above the line is salvation below the line is heathenism. We all start below the line. If our imaginary friend is trying to work for his salvation and every good work brought him closer to the line, could he eventually cross the line through good works? No! The best that he could do would be to bump up against the bottom of the line. If works do not save us, how are we saved? The answer to that is faith! Only by faith can a person cross the line.

Suppose the man put his faith in Christ and is now comfortably sitting on the salvation (top) side of the line, how would he ever go back – or backslide? Here is where we evangelicals often mix our doctrine of grace with a doctrine of works. We understand that we cannot be saved by works but for some reason we think we can be unsaved by works. Subsequently, when we see someone who once lived openly for the Lord who is now obviously not living for the Lord, we call him or her backslidden, when we should probably call him or her a carnal Christian. We cannot lose our salvation by bad works any more than we could gain it by good works. However, a person can lose their salvation by doing the opposite of what they did to get saved.

We are saved by faith. That is the Greek word *"pistis."* The only way to be unsaved is through the opposite of faith, which is the word apostasy *"apostasia."* However, the root word for *apostasia* is *apostaseeon* which means "divorce." You could say that carnal Christians do not necessarily have a good marriage with the Lord, but they have taken the vow and are indeed married.

A person does not become married by just doing good things for the one they want to marry, any more than doing good, religious things can wed you to Christ. Subsequently, neither does he get unmarried by doing bad things. Bad things may lead to a divorce, but the bad action itself will not un-marry a couple.

The Bible talks about the great apostasy (unfaith) in 2 Thessalonians chapter 2 and verse 3. We cannot have unfaith unless there was first faith. The world is not in an apostate condition or state. The world is in an unregenerate state. The world cannot commit apostasy. To be unregenerate is to have never had faith. Therefore, it is possible to lose our salvation but it is not simple. It doesn't happen just because someone got caught up in a habit or something sinful. A person would need to be just as deliberate about leaving God as spouses are when they divorce. Divorce is a deliberate action with full knowledge of what is taking place. To backslide would be a willful turning away from faith. We would have to declare that we no longer even believe in God to be considered backslidden.

The Three Classifications of Man

Having said all that let's now begin to look at what an overcomer is and what a carnal Christian is. Some have accused the Partial Rapture theory as making classes out of Christians. They believe that to say Overcomers vs. Carnal Christians creates classes of Christians. Actually, Paul the Apostle is the one who classified Christians. There are actually three clasifications of man in the following verses.

1 Corinthians 2:14-3:3 "The man without the Spirit does not accept the things that come from the Spirit of God, for they are foolishness to him, and he cannot understand them, because they are Spiritually discerned. (15) The Spiritual man makes judgments about all things, but he himself is not subject to any man's judgment: (16) "For who has known the mind of the Lord that he may instruct him?" But we have the mind of Christ."
1 Corinthians 3:1 "Brothers, I could not address you as Spiritual but as worldly-mere infants in Christ. (2) I gave you milk, not solid food, for you were not yet ready for it. Indeed, you are still not ready. (3) You are still worldly."

1. The Natural Man - **1 Corinthians 2:14, "The man without the Spirit."** The Greek language uses the word psuchikos to describe this man. Psuchikos breaks down into two parts: "*Psuchi*" and "*kos.*" Psuchi is where we get the word Psych from. The psyche of man relates to his mind. The natural man does not accept the things of God for he cannot understand them. The things of God are spiritually discerned and the natural man only relates to his five senses. If he can smell, hear, taste, see or feel it, then he can believe it. This is a man who does not know Christ at all. He is unregenerate. The suffix of this word is "kos," which basically means "in the image of." So the natural man is in the image of his five senses. He has never had a born-again experience.

2. The Spiritual Man - **1 Corinthians 2:15 "The Spiritual man makes judgments about all things, but he himself is not subject to any man's judgment."**

The Greek word for spiritual is "*pneumatikos,*" which means non-carnal. It also breaks down into two parts. The first part is the word "*pneumati.*" Pneuma is where we get the word "Spirit" from. A pneumatic wrench is an air wrench. Any pneumatic tool is a tool powered by air, or in this case, Spirit. Again the suffix "*kos*" means in the image of. Therefore the Spiritual man is a man in the image of the Spirit of God. He has allowed himself to be transformed by the renewing of his mind. This is the type of man we all want to be. The Spiritual man is the overcomer.

3. The Worldly Man - **1 Corinthians 3:1 "Brothers, I could not address you as Spiritual but as worldly-mere infants in Christ."** The word "worldly" in the Greek is "*Sarkinos*." This word means flesh or carcass. The whole of the word means, in the image of his flesh, which is the definition of a carnal Christian. Notice that Paul refers to them as brothers, subsequently, placing them in the family of God, but still worldly minded. In this sense they are in a different category than the natural man. They are born-again but do not have spiritual pursuits. They do not have spiritual disciplines. Prayer in their life is rare and studying the Word is unheard of. They lack passion for the Lord. They are happy just to be saved. All through the New Testament we find challenges for us to grow up. In the book of Hebrews chapter 5 the writer is talking about how by now these disciples should be teachers, but instead they still someone to teach them. Then in verse thirteen he calls them babes in Christ. The word 'babe' in the Greek means carnal.

Some have compared the spiritual man and the carnal man to hot air balloons. Both are full of hot air (which in this case would be a type of the Holy Spirit), however, the spiritual balloon has broken free from the earth's grip, whereas the carnal balloon is still tethered to the earth. How then can a tethered balloon rise up to meet the Lord in the air? He must break free from his ties to this world. Paul's final word to the carnal Christian is "you are still worldly," or, you can't break free from the love of this world.

The rapture of the Church is for the overcomer (Spiritual man), not because he is more special to God, but rather because Jesus is looking for people to rule and reign with him in the Millennium. This is not God creating two classes of Christians – this is God giving us the choice of the kind of life we want to live, with hundreds of warnings to live the right way.

The carnal Christian will remain on earth to possibly gain the position of overcomer through martyrdom. We must all pay a price in order to rule and reign with Christ. The overcomer is willing to pay the price during this life. He has Spiritual pursuits and objectives. His life's goal is to glorify and beautify the Bride of Christ. The carnal Christian chooses not to pay the price today, and cannot be convinced of the importance of Spiritual pursuits and will, afterwards, pay the price during the Tribulation if he wants to rule with Christ.

Chapter Four

The First Qualifier of the Overcomer

You Must Live a Spirit Filled Life!

For the next 5 chapters we are going to look at the 5 qualifiers of the overcomer.

Matthew 25:1-6 "At that time the kingdom of heaven will be like ten virgins who took their lamps and went out to meet the bridegroom. (2) Five of them were foolish and five were wise. (3) The foolish ones took their lamps but did not take any oil with them. (4) The wise, however, took oil in jars along with their lamps. (5) The bridegroom was a long time in coming, and they all became drowsy and fell asleep. (6) "At midnight the cry rang out: 'Here's the bridegroom! Come out to meet him! (7) "Then all the virgins woke up and trimmed their lamps. (8) The foolish ones said to the wise, `Give us some of your oil; our lamps are going out.' (9) "`No,' they replied, `there may not be enough for both us and you. Instead, go to those who sell oil and buy some for yourselves.' (10) "But while they were on their way to buy the oil, the bridegroom arrived. The virgins who were ready went in with him to the wedding banquet. And the door was shut. (11) "Later the others also came. `Sir! Sir!' they said. `Open the door for us!' (12) "But he replied, `I tell you the truth, I don't know you.' (13) "Therefore keep watch, because you do not know the day or the hour."

Keep watch because you do not know the day or the hour. What is there to watch for if the rapture is automatic with salvation? If being saved means we are going automatically, what is the purpose of a teaching that warns Christians to live ready? What it means is this: the rapture does not deal with our redemption but rather addresses the Spiritual quality of our lives,

This is a direct warning to the Church. Keep watch because you do not know the day or the hour. Some people I have been reading on this subject still want to believe that this warning goes out to the non-Christians. I don't believe that is supported at all by the scriptures. These are warnings for the Church. The parable begins with the words of Jesus as he says; "*At that time the kingdom of heaven will be like ten virgins who took their lamps and went out to meet the bridegroom.*" This is a reference to the kingdom of heaven, which never includes the lost.

Ephesians 2:1-2 "As for you, you were dead in your transgressions and sins, (2) in which you used to live when you followed the ways of this world and of the ruler of the kingdom of the air, the Spirit who is now at work in those who are disobedient."

The Bible talks about the kingdom of God or the kingdom of this world (air). Those who are dead in trespasses and sins follow the ways of this world. They follow the ruler of the kingdom of the air which, of course, is a reference to the prince of the power of the air – the old enemy.

Ephesians 5:5 "For of this you can be sure: No immoral, impure or greedy person — such a man is an idolater — has any inheritance in the kingdom of Christ and of God."

No one on this list will be included in the kingdom of heaven. Therefore, when this parable starts off by referring to the kingdom of heaven, it does not include those of the kingdom of this world. It is a reference to the people in the kingdom of God.

Five virgins were ready, five were not. They were all virgins and they all had a lamp. The lamp is symbolic of salvation. That puts them all in the same category.

Psalms 18:28 "You, O Lord, keep my lamp burning; my God turns my darkness into light."

God turns my darkness into light. God turning the darkness of our life into light is a reference to when we get saved. Notice that there is a plea for God to keep the lamp burning – signifying there is a possibility that the lamp might lose its ability to shine. It is not a reference to losing salvation. It stresses the possibility of being in possession of the lamp without it being able to light the way.

The lamp is a symbol of salvation. All ten of the virgins had the lamp but only those with oil in their lamps were able to go with the groom. The big question here is: does the oil represent the Holy Spirit? Not entirely, because to be in possession of the lamp is to be in possession of the Holy Spirit. All Christians gain the Holy Spirit at salvation, but there is a great difference between being in possession of the Holy Spirit and living a Spirit filled life. I believe the oil represents the Spirit filled life or the life of the overcomer. Not only are we to possess the lamp, but we must allow it to shine.

Matthew 5:14-16 "You are the light of the world. A city on a hill cannot be hidden. (15) Neither do people light a lamp and put it under a bowl. Instead they put it on its stand, and it gives light to everyone in the house. (16) In the same way, let your light shine before men, that they may see your good deeds and praise your Father in heaven."

The whole idea of the foolish virgins was that they had salvation, but their lamps did not shine.

Ephesians 5:18 "Do not get drunk on wine, which leads to debauchery. Instead, be filled with the Spirit."

The little phrase, "be filled with the Spirit," in the Greek reads, "keep on being filled." In other words, we leak. Our salvation does not leak out of us, but the fullness of the

48

Spirit can. Remember how the Psalmist said, "**O Lord, keep my lamp burning?**"

We are to continually be filled with the Spirit. The foolish virgin's lamps were not filled. We Pentecostals want this to be a reference to the Baptism of the Holy Spirit, but I'm not sure we can do that. We all receive the Holy Spirit when we get saved. Rather than calling it the Baptism of the Holy Spirit, we should probably call it the potential that the Baptism gives us. The foolish virgins were not witnesses of the goodness of God. We need to live a Spirit filled life in the same way that the virgins needed an oil-filled lamp.

Some have said that this cannot be the Holy Spirit because the foolish virgins were instructed to go out and buy the oil and we cannot purchase the Holy Spirit. That is correct, however, not all parables parallel exactly.

Purchasing the oil is most likely a reference to the price we pay to live the way we should. Otherwise, it would indicate that there is something we could go out and buy in order to make it in the rapture.

Revelation 3:18 "I counsel you to buy from me gold refined in the fire, so you can become rich; and white clothes to wear."

Here we have the Holy Spirit counseling the Church of Laodecia to go out and buy good works. Gold refined in the fire is a direct reference to the Judgement Seat of Christ when all our works pass through the fire. Only the gold and precious stones pass through the fire without burning up. Can any of us buy good works? Can anyone become an overcomer by giving money to a worthy cause? No! However, many overcomers give to worthy causes because of who they are, not in an effort to become something they are not. We must pay a price to live in such a way that our works will pass through the fire and not burn up.

The foolish virgins being instructed to go out to buy oil is only figuratively speaking. Then the next question is: does this mean that only the people who have the Baptism of the Holy Spirit are going in the rapture? That question is easily answered. The rapture is for the overcomer and the Baptism of the Holy Spirit is merely a means to become what God wants us to be, but it is no guarantee.

There are many "tongue-talking believers" who are quite carnal and not living as overcomers. However, the difficulty comes in trying to be an overcomer without the Baptism. I would never preach that you couldn't be an overcoming Christian without the Baptism, but why try? I believe history is filled with people who led overcoming lives without what we call the Baptism but why try? Why work so hard at something that God has given us to empower us. Overcomers seek all that God has for them. They take the Apostle Paul's admonition to, earnestly pursue spiritual gifts, seriously.

The very Spirit of the overcomer is one who longs for Christ. He looks for Him. He wants everything that Christ has for him. Only the carnal mind would struggle with the idea of gaining something to assist them in becoming an overcomer. Lets look at the Bible's description of an overcomer.

1 John 5:3-5 "This is love for God: to obey his commands. And his commands are not burdensome, (4) for everyone born of God overcomes the world. This is the victory that has overcome the world, even our faith. (5) Who is it that overcomes the world? Only he who believes that Jesus is the Son of God."

I believe that every believer starts off their relationship with God as an overcomer in the sense that they overcame the world by surrendering their life to Christ. This verse does not address the issue of living an overcoming life, but rather how the surrender of our life to Christ has given us the victory over this world.

We cannot discount Paul's teaching about the Spiritual man and the carnal man, indicating that it is possible to have overcome the world regarding salvation and yet live with an attraction to this world, or as the parable of the ten virgins teaches, live foolishly. Without – what – is it impossible to please God?   Faith! This is the victory that has overcome the world, even our faith. Without faith we cannot maintain the Spiritual life. The carnal Christian does not pursue great faith and has reverted back to putting his trust in this world. That is foolish living.

Five of the virgins lived foolishly. The Greek word for foolish is *moros*, which is where we get our word moron from. The word means heedless. Those who live foolishly will one day will find that they were warned over and over but did not heed the warnings.   This is an especially important definition in light of this parable, which is a warning. The overcomer heeds warnings – the foolish do not. Subsequently, they overcame the world when they came into possession of the lamp (salvation) but they did not live a life of faith, which by definition is foolishness. How foolish is it to believe God for your salvation, but not believe him for your provisions or your sustenance?

Betrothed!

We are in the engagement period with Christ. We are the betrothed of Christ.   An ancient Jewish custom teaches some important things concerning the overcoming bride. The tradition was that once a Jewish couple was engaged to be married they would separate during that period of time so that the groom could go and prepare a house (Jesus has left us on earth while He prepares a place for us in His Fathers house).

The bride agreed to sleep each night with her window open. She is longing for his appearing and every night at midnight she would get out of bed to listen for the call of the groom (that is the longing heart of a pray-er).

Once the house was prepared then the groom would come into town, but he himself would not go to the window. Instead he would send his friends to the window and they would shout, "Behold the bridegroom cometh," (that is what preachers, prophets, and anyone used by the Holy Spirit does).

That would be like the warning. That is what this parable is - a call to live ready. As soon as she heard the shout she would get up, trim the lamp, get dressed and be ready. Then the friends of the groom would lead the bride through the dark streets to the groom. That is why her lamp needed to be able to shine. She is walking through a dark world. Then he would take her away for one week.

John 14:1-4 "Do not let your hearts be troubled. Trust in God; trust also in me. (2) In my Father's house are many rooms; if it were not so, I would have told you. I am going there to prepare a place for you. (3) And if I go

and prepare a place for you, I will come back and take you to be with me that you also may be where I am. (4) You know the way to the place where I am going."

Jesus is coming for his bride to take her with him for one week which is equivalent to seven years (more about that in chapter 10), the amount of time the tribulation period will take on earth.

Chapter Five

The Second Qualifier of an Overcomer

Must be living a purified life!

There are several warnings in the scripture that the overcomer should heed. The second warning we are going to look at is that we must live a purified life. Keep in mind we are talking about the rapture as one of the rewards we get for living as an overcomer. We are not talking about salvation.

The Purified Life

1 John 3:2-3 "Dear friends, now we are children of God, and what we will be has not yet been made known. But we know that when he appears, we shall be like him, for we shall see him as he is. (3) Everyone who has this hope in him purifies himself, just as he is pure."

We are pure by the blood of Christ unto salvation. The blood of Christ has gained our salvation. But that is dealing with salvation, not the rapture of the Church.

Titus 2:11-14 "For the grace of God that brings salvation has appeared to all men. (12) It teaches us to say "No" to ungodliness and worldly passions, and to live self-controlled, upright and godly lives in this present age,

(13) while we wait for the blessed hope-the glorious appearing of our great God and Savior, Jesus Christ, (14) who gave himself for us to redeem us from all wickedness and to purify for himself a people that are his very own, eager to do what is good."

Do you see what he is saying? We are pure through the blood of Christ; we are saved, but that has nothing to do with the rapture. The rapture is for those who allow their own purification to teach them to deny ungodliness, worldliness, and to live sensibility and righteously, looking for Christ in this present age. It's the looking for Christ that purifies us.

History has shown us that whenever the Church loses sight of the imminent return of Christ, it loses sight of the significance of holy living. Holy living is nearly laughed at today by the Church because we think it is a works issue. And it would be a works issue if we were only dealing with the salvation of man. But we are not – we are dealing with the rapture as a reward for right living.

The word "imminent" means that which hovers above us, which could drop at any moment. What I mean by losing sight of the imminent return of Christ is that of being lulled to sleep, Spiritually. Don't you think that has happened to the American Church? We are so taken up with ourselves we could never be taken up by Jesus. It comes down to this: we must be taken up with Jesus long before we can be taken up by Jesus.

1 John 2:28 "And now, dear children, continue in him, so that when he appears we may be confident and unashamed before him at his coming."

This verse has the condition and warning about his return. It's found in three words, "**continue in Him.**" Continuing in Him so that we will be unashamed when he appears, implies that if we do not continue in Him we will be ashamed at his appearing. What does it mean to continue (live) in Him? The answer can be found in the same chapter of 1 John:

1 John 2:6 Whoever claims to live in him must walk as Jesus did."

The word "live" in this verse and the word "continue" in the previous verse have the same exact Greek meaning, which is to abide. If anyone claims to abide in Him, he must walk as Jesus walked. WWJD. If you are wondering if you abide in him, just ask yourself if Jesus would do the things you do?

When we walk as he walked we live with the hope that when He appears we shall be like Him. This means more than us instantly conforming to His character at the time of His coming. This verse is telling us that the "depth" or "impact" of His appearing is decided by our Christ-likeness before His appearing. Verse 3 brings this out:

1 John 3:3 "Everyone who has this hope in him purifies himself, just as he is pure."

Everyone who has the hope of being like Him, when He appears, has that hope, because of his or her pure heart. When you live with the hope of being like Him, you purify your own heart in the process, because you walk as He walked. Subsequently, you purify yourself just as He is pure.

It takes purity of heart to be able to "see." Revelation comes through our ability to see, spiritually. And our walk relates to our ability to see because it purifies us. **"Everyone who has the hope of seeing Him**." Isn't that an interesting phrase. Here is what I want to propose. The rapture, though an actual event, will also be spiritual, and only be experienced by those with the ability to see spiritually. I do not believe the carnal Christian, nor those who are in the world, will even see Jesus when He comes in the clouds. Blessed are the pure in heart for they shall see God. Purity of heart brings revelation.

Chapter Six

The Third Qualifier of the Overcomer

You must be living a life of Faith!

In Luke chapter 18, Jesus teaches his disciples a parable:

Luke 18:1-8 "Then Jesus told his disciples a parable to show them that they should always pray and not give up. (2) He said: "In a certain town there was a judge who neither feared God nor cared about men.   (3) And there was a widow in that town who kept coming to him with the plea, 'Grant me justice against my adversary.' (4) "For some time he refused. But finally he said to himself, 'Even though I don't fear God or care about men,   (5) yet because this widow keeps bothering me, I will see that she gets justice, so that she won't eventually wear me out with her coming!'" (6) And the Lord said, "Listen to what the unjust judge says.   (7) And will not God bring about justice for his chosen ones, who cry out to him day and night? Will he keep putting them off? (8) I tell you, he will see that they get justice, and quickly. However, when the Son of Man comes, will he find faith on the earth?"

Look at how this parable concludes. In verse 8 it says, "*However, when the Son of Man comes, will he find faith on the earth*?" When Jesus comes, he will take those of faith, the overcomers.   Did you know that prayer relates to faith? It has to. Why pray unless you believe, or you could reverse the logic and say, *"Why pray since you don't believe?"* Prayer and faith go hand in hand. Prayer is obviously not the only way to display faith, but you cannot live by faith without prayer. Those who believe, pray; those who do not believe, worry. The scriptures say, **"Be anxious for nothing but in everything by prayer and petition let your requests be made known."** The Bible basically says that prayerlessness is sinful in its nature.

The lack of prayer, no matter how you cut it, is from the lack of faith. To say that you have faith and, yet, not have a prayer life makes no practical sense. If you really believe, then pray. God will honor your faith when you pray. A life of faith is simply a life that pleases God.

In Hebrews 11:5-6 we read, "By faith Enoch was taken from this life, so that he did not experience death; he could not be found, because God had taken him away. For before he was taken, he was commended as one who pleased God. (6)And without faith it is impossible to please God..."

Before he was taken up, he obtained the testimony that he pleased God. You cannot please God without faith. Do you think carnal Christians please God with the lifestyle they live? Before the rapture happens we must attain the same type of testimony. We must please God to be an overcomer. Enoch's experience is a type of the rapture. And he was taken, because he pleased God. He had obtained that witness. Without faith, it is impossible to please God.

Revelation 22:17 "The Spirit and the bride say, "Come!" And let him who hears say, "Come!"

The nature of the Bride, (the Bride is the overcomer) is to desire or long, not only for justice, but, also, for the groom Himself. We are to continually cry out for the Messiah to come and take us because we want to be with Him. The more we pray for His soon return, the more it will affect how we live. If we live with the thought of Him returning any day, and pray to that end, it will change how we live. To not pray for his return is to be content with life here on earth, which usually indicates carnality.

Let's reconsider the parable Jesus associated with his return. He starts it off by saying that men should always pray and not give up. Then He brings in a woman, who won't quit asking for justice. She finally gets her request because she would never stop asking. Then he associates this with His return. There are two things for us to consider here. First of all, she wouldn't quit asking; she displayed her faith by her continual asking, or praying. Secondly, it has to do with what she was asking for, which was justice.

Luke 18:6-7 "And the Lord said, "Listen to what the unjust judge says. (7) And will not God bring about justice for his chosen ones, who cry out to him day and night? Will he keep putting them off?"

We live in an unjust world. Injustice is what is causing all the hurt and calamity we see. The Lord longs to bring justice to this world. However, as Christians and, particularly, overcoming Christians, we can live above the injustice knowing that eventually God will balance the books. Miguel de Molinos, founder of a movement called the Quietist, (because of his emphasis on contemplative prayer) was convicted by the Catholic Church in 1687 on some trumped up charges. While being led away to his prison cell (where he eventually died) he cried out to his accusers, *"We shall meet again, in the judgment day; and then it will appear on which side, on yours or mine, that the truth is."* The only acceptable attitude we can have is futuristic. We must look at the mistreatments we face as one day being balanced by God Himself.

The whole purpose of the Tribulation is that God has a controversy with the nations. It is a part of God balancing the books. The final correction will be the Great White Throne Judgment, when the book of life will be opened and anyone whose name is not found therein will go into an eternity without God.

Chapter Seven

The Fourth Qualifier of an Overcomer

Must be a Christian working in the service of the Lord!

Mark 13:32-37 **"No one knows about that day or hour, not even the angels in heaven, nor the Son, but only the Father. (33) Be on guard! Be alert! You do not know when that time will come.** **(34) It's like a man going away:** (*This would be Jesus*) **He leaves his house and puts his servants in charge, each with his assigned task,** (*he gave each of us something to do*) **and tells the one at the door** (*The Holy Spirit*) **to keep watch.** (*the Holy Spirit is watching all of us*) **(35) "Therefore keep watch because you do not know when the owner of the house will come back** (*that relates to verse 32*)**-whether in the evening, or at midnight, or when the rooster crows, or at dawn. (36) If he comes suddenly, do not let him find you sleeping.** (*not doing the work of the Lord*) **(37) What I say to you, I say to everyone: 'Watch!'"** (*Emphasis mine*)

This is the first Qualifier with such a direct warning. Three different times he gives a warning. **Verse 33, "Be on guard! Be alert!" Verse 35, "Keep watch." And verse 37, "What I say to you I say to everyone: Watch!"** Again, I have to ask, "What is the purpose of a warning, if it is not needed? If every born-again person is going to go in the rapture automatically, why does the scripture give stern warnings about watching?"

God has a work for all of us. What would that be? What is it God wants us to do? Jesus did not teach these parables just to have something to do. He is making an emphatic point here. Keep in mind, it's not just that Jesus wants us to be busy people, He wants us to be passionate people. In this case, it is passion for the advancement of the kingdom of God. The very fact that most Churches in America have to work hard to get people to serve in the Church proves that we do not have the mindset of an overcomer.

Serving God doesn't take place exclusively in the Church. Certainly you can serve Him there, but you can serve him on the job, in your home, and as you shop. You can also serve him as you enjoy recreation. Find out what it is God would have you do, and do it. For the sake of reigning with Him, do it!

I remember having a wonderful experience during RPM. RPM stands for **R**adical **P**rayer **M**eeting. It was a men's prayer meeting we conducted in our Church for many years. This particular prayer meeting was profound in that God was in it – the revelation I received was not so profound. There was a worship song playing in the background. When it came to the chorus of the song it repeated over and over that God wants to save, restore, and heal. I was simply overwhelmed with the idea the God hurts over who are hurting and that the Church needs to go back to what God has called it to do, which is to help people find their salvation, restoration, and healing.

There are many marriages that need restoration in our town, and in the Church. There are healings that need to take place. We are the Church; we have been given an assignment, and the Holy Spirit is watching to see if we are doing our task.

So, the scripture says watch for his return. Watching keeps us working for the Lord. If we lose sight of watching for Him, if we go to sleep spiritually, then we tend to no longer see the significance of serving God. Watch over your work. Use great care in protecting the task God has given you. This is incredibly important to the Lord. If we prove ourselves faithful over the little things, God will make us a ruler over many things.

Remember how in the parable in Matthew 25 about the talents? The one who did nothing for God, even though God gave him talents, did not enter into the joy of the Lord. The warning to the Church is that the Holy Spirit is watching.

Therefore, we must keep watch ourselves, because we do not know when the owner of the house will come back.

Chapter Eight

The Fifth Qualifier of the Overcomer

You must be looking for Jesus!

Hebrews 9:28 "So Christ was sacrificed once to take away the sins of many people; and he will appear a second time, not to bear sin, but to bring salvation to those who are waiting for him."

The grammatical construction of this verse indicates this: If we do not look for Him we will not see him. Overcomers look for Him. Christ is coming for those who eagerly await His return.

The idea in this verse about looking for him would be like you actually going to a window and putting your hands around your eyes so that you can see farther, looking in anticipation. I remember as a kid when my grandparents were going to come for a visit, (they would drive all the way across the whole state of South Dakota), I would literally sit on our couch waiting all day long, looking at every car that drove by, hoping each car would be the one that turned into our driveway. I just couldn't wait. It was really quite funny, because I would wait all day for them to get there, but once they got there I realized they were too old to play with me, so I would go out and find my friends.

Whether we are talking about the overcomer, or those who have been overcome, we are talking about the Spirit of the person. The Spirit of the overcomer longs for Christ to appear. Anybody can love Jesus. There is any number of people, who do not know Christ, who claim to love Him. Loving Him is easy; longing for Him, working for Him, living by faith, and serving Him are traits of the overcomer.

At this point I'm going to interject some thoughts about the wedding supper of the Lamb and how that relates to longing for His appearing.

Wedding Supper

Revelation 19:9 "Then the angel said to me, "Write this: Blessed are those who are invited to the wedding supper of the Lamb!" And he added, "These are the true words of God."

Who will be at the supper? The overcomer. The nominal Christian will not be there. Apparently the wedding supper of the Lamb will take place at the end of the Tribulation period, so that all those who died during the Tribulation can have an opportunity to be there. Those who attend the supper are those whose works did not burn up at the Beam Seat Judgment.

Revelation 22:17, "The Spirit and the Bride say come Lord Jesus."

That verse could also read; "**The Spirit of the Bride says come Lord Jesus.**" You cannot separate the Spirit from the bride. The true bride waits eagerly for her love. The bride says come – the carnal Christian does not. The carnal Christian loves this life and all the comforts it offers. All of this comes down to the spirit of a person. An overcomer is not necessarily someone who has accomplished perfection in this life. It's someone who has a right spirit; someone who continually picks him or herself up when they fall, and continues on the path towards God.

Making Herself Ready

Revelation 19:7 "Let us rejoice and be glad and give him glory! For the wedding of the Lamb has come, and his bride has made herself ready. (8) Fine linen, bright and clean, was given her to wear." (Fine linen stands for the righteous acts of the saints.)

Is the bride ready? If salvation has made us ready for the wedding of the Lamb, then these verses we just read are not necessary. Three things make the bride ready - salvation, the Holy Spirit, and the wedding gown. Assuming you have the lamp of salvation and the oil of the Holy Spirit, let's look at why the wedding gown is necessary.

The verse says that the bride makes herself ready for the wedding. If salvation is the only criteria for participation in the wedding supper of the Lamb, there would be absolutely nothing she could do to make herself ready. We cannot earn salvation however, what we see here is that she does have a role in her readiness, and that relates to her wedding gown.

Matthew 22:1-14 "Jesus spoke to them again in parables, saying: (2)"The kingdom of heaven is like a king who prepared a wedding banquet for his son. (3) He sent his servants to those who had been invited to the banquet to tell them to come, but they refused to come... (9) Go to the street corners and invite to the banquet anyone you find.' (10) So the servants went out into the streets and gathered all the people they could find, both good and bad, and the wedding hall was filled with guests. (11) "But when the king came in to see the guests, he noticed a man there who was not wearing wedding clothes. (12) `Friend,' he asked, `how did you get in here without wedding clothes?' The man was speechless. (13) "Then the king told the attendants, `Tie him hand and foot, and throw him outside, into the darkness, where there will be weeping and gnashing of teeth.' (14) "For many are invited, but few are chosen."

The man did not have wedding clothes. Subsequently, he could not participate. Did you know that verse 14, "**many are invited but few are chosen**," is relating to the rapture of the Church, not salvation. The bride making herself ready is a direct reference to her wedding gown. The gown is made up of her righteous acts. Do you see the role that works plays here? Works have nothing to do with our salvation, but they play a big role as to whether or not we are a part of the wedding supper of the Lamb. Righteous acts are works. Every little thing we do for Jesus is another stitch in our gown.

2 Timothy 4:8 "Now there is in store for me the crown of righteousness, which the Lord, the righteous Judge, will award to me on that day-and not only to me, but also to all who have longed for his appearing."

Righteous living is related to longing for His appearing. The more a person looks for Christ to come soon, the more he tends to work for the Lord. It's really quite simple - if I fully believe that I could stand before the Judgement Seat of Christ soon, then I am going to want to store up as many treasures in heaven as I can now. All of those treasures in heaven are acts of righteousness. Subsequently, if you are not looking for His return, you will not see Him because you don't put any energy into living for Him, you don't work as you could for him; you do not have a wedding gown to wear that is fit to wear.

Chapter Nine

Foreshadows & Crowns

Some of the critics of the partial rapture theory believe it confuses grace with works, stating that, if not everyone goes in the rapture, this teaching suggests that we have to earn our salvation. That comes from the false premise that the rapture is inclusive with salvation.

If you believe that every Christian goes in the rapture, and then hear a teaching that says some may not go because they did not live an overcoming life, your natural conclusion would point to salvation by works. But it doesn't. Salvation is by the blood of Christ, only. However, there is no indication in the Word that leads us to believe that, if we are saved, we automatically go in the rapture. That has always been an assumption, because we equated the rapture with being saved. In fact, there are far more Bible verses that point to the fact that some don't make it, than there are that indicate all those who name the name of Christ as their own go in the Pre-trib rapture.

Luke 17:30-35 "It will be just like this on the day the Son of Man is revealed. (31) On that day no one who is on the roof of his house, with his goods inside, should go down to get them. Likewise, no one in the field should go back for anything. (32) Remember Lot's wife! (33)

Whoever tries to keep his life will lose it, and whoever loses his life will preserve it. (34) I tell you, on that night two people will be in one bed; one will be taken and the other left. (35) Two women will be grinding grain together; one will be taken and the other left."

These verses start off by basically telling us to not live for the things of this world. If you are on the roof of your house and you see the Lord coming, don't worry about what's in the house. You cannot be taken up with the things of this world, and be taken up with Jesus at the same time. Verse 33 brings that out vividly.

Two people will be in one bed; one will be taken and the other left. This is not a picture of a Christian and a non-Christian. These are two of the same spirit. The little phrase, "in one bed," tells us that they had the same heart. However, only one of them goes in the rapture. Two women will be grinding grain together; one will be taken and the other left. Again we have the same situation. They were of one heart, grinding grain together, one is taken, one is left. There are far more illustrations of believers being left behind than there are illustrations of all Christians going.

Some might ask, "How do you know the two in one bed, and the two in the field are of one heart?" It's because of verse 32, which is right in the middle of this teaching, he says, **"Remember Lot's wife."** Lot's deliverance from

73

Sodom and Gomorrah is a type of the Pre-trib rapture of the Church. They leave just before the destruction comes. What do we remember about Lot's wife? She did not go with the rest of her family. She had the same heart as the rest of her family; she was a believer in God, and yet she did not make it out of the destruction because of her draw to this world. She looked back, indicating she had a longing for her carnal existence, and turned into a pillar of salt.

The only other way to look at these teachings is to say that they are all examples of believers going and non-believers staying. If that were the case, what is the purpose of a warning? We all know that the non-Christian is not going to go in the rapture, so who are the warnings going out to? These warnings were written to those who have the hope of going in the rapture. Remember Lot's wife! That's the lesson. She was a believer, who did not make it, because of her attraction to this world.

Once you accept the fact that the rapture is not inclusive with salvation, you can see that there is no blending of works and grace at all. We are saved by grace. That is all there is to it. The rapture comes by works, period! To miss the rapture does not mean you are not a Christian. It simply means you lived foolishly and did not live an overcoming life. If you were to die today as a carnal Christian, you would go to heaven, but you would not rule and reign with Christ during the Millennium.

There are also critics who say that God would not divide His family. He would not leave some here and take others with Him. Really! Is not the family divided right now? Are not uncounted millions of believers who have died in the faith, in the presence of God now, while we are still on earth? Do we consider that unfair? No! We simply realize that that is how it is. At the time of the rapture the carnal Christian is not going to say, "*This is not fair, why did I get left, I should be in heaven along with everybody else.*" I doubt very much that his reaction will be that of pride. If anything, he will be humbled by the fact that he was left behind and will accept his plight and, ultimately, die as a martyr, if he wants to gain an overcomer status.

Remember, God is not fair; God is just. Nowhere does the Bible call God fair – it calls Him just. If God were fair then he would have to treat all people the same, which would mean that everybody who is born-again would go in the rapture. But God is just. God does what is right for each one of us.

Foreshadows

1 Corinthians 10:1-6 For I do not want you to be ignorant of the fact, brothers, that our forefathers were all under the cloud and that they all passed through the sea. (2) They were all baptized into Moses in the cloud and in the sea. (3) They all ate the same spiritual food (4) and drank the same spiritual drink; for they drank from the Spiritual rock that accompanied them, and that rock was Christ. (5) Nevertheless, God was not pleased with most of them; their bodies were scattered over the desert. (6) Now these things occurred as examples to keep us from setting our hearts on evil things as they did.

1 Corinthians 10:11-12 These things happened to them as examples and were written down as warnings for us, on whom the fulfillment of the ages has come. (12) So, if you think you are standing firm, be careful that you don't fall!

Jesus is talking about Israel's wilderness wanderings and how these things happened to them as examples for you and me. Isn't that an incredible thought! Israel went through what she did because you and I needed an example to look at, so that we would not fall into the same trap. And that trap was that of thinking that once we are saved we no longer have a thing to worry about regarding the rapture. Verse 12 states, "So if you think you are standing firm, be careful." This is a direct reference to going in the rapture. We could paraphrase this verse to say; *"So, if you think your salvation is a guarantee to make the rapture, be careful."*

Keep in mind, the 40 years in the desert is a lesson for us about the rapture. To deny this parallel is to overthrow inspiration; to ignore the parallel is to silence the Scripture. To admit the parallel is to reveal a potential peril to the believer in Christ. We cannot just ignore the lessons of the Bible. We cannot simply write them off as only being pertinent to another generation. If we deny this parallel, we suggest that the Bible is not inspired by God. If we ignore it, we silence the scriptures. However, if we see it, we also see the lesson it has for us all.

Here is the great lesson about the wandering. We will take it right from 1 Corinthians 10: **"Our forefathers were all under the cloud**." That refers to the covering of their sin. The blood of the Lamb, which was put on their doorpost the night of the Passover, redeemed them. Verse 2 says, **"They were all baptized into Moses in the cloud and in the sea**." This is symbolic of water Baptism and their separation from the world. **"They all ate the same spiritual food and drank the same spiritual drink**." This is symbolic of their communion with Christ, even in the desert thousands of years before His birth. So here we have them saved, baptized, and in communion with Christ. Yet only two of them enter the promise land. Do you know who those two were? We read of them in Numbers 32.

Numbers 32:11-12 `Because they have not followed me wholeheartedly, not one of the men twenty years old or more who came up out of Egypt will see the land I promised on oath to Abraham, Isaac and Jacob— (12) not one except Caleb son of Jephunneh the Kenizzite and Joshua son of Nun, for they followed the LORD wholeheartedly.'

Out of that entire original generation, which was delivered from Egypt, only Joshua and Caleb make it to the promise land. The promise land is symbolic of the Millennial Reign, not heaven. It was a land flowing with milk and honey. It was to be a place of rest from their lifetime of wandering through the desert.

Entering into His Rest

Hebrews 3:7-11 "So, as the Holy Spirit says: "Today, if you hear his voice, (8) do not harden your hearts as you did in the rebellion, during the time of testing in the desert, (9) where your fathers tested and tried me and for forty years saw what I did. (10) That is why I was angry with that generation, and I said, 'Their hearts are always going astray, and they have not known my ways.' (11) So I declared on oath in my anger, 'They shall never enter my rest.'"

The "rest" referred to in verse 11 is the Millennial Reign of Christ. The Millennium is symbolic of the seventh day of creation, where God rested. We have had six thousand years on this earth, which is symbolic of the first six days of creation, and on the seventh day, or the final "thousand years," God rested. Those who were tried and failed did not enter into God's rest. They will not rule and reign with Christ. They will not live again until the thousand years are finished.

Joshua and Caleb entered into God's rest because of faith. We just read in Hebrews chapter three that God did not allow the Israelites into the promise land because of their unbelief. In that light, look at what Hebrews chapter four says.

Hebrews 4:1-6 "Therefore, since the promise of entering his rest still stands, let us be careful that none of you be found to have fallen short of it. (2)For we also have had the gospel preached to us, just as they did; but the message they heard was of no value to them, because those who heard did not combine it with faith. (3) Now we who have believed enter that rest, just as God has said, "So I declared on oath in my anger, `They shall never enter my rest.'" And yet his work has been finished since the creation of the world. (4) For somewhere he has spoken about the seventh day in these words: "And on the seventh day God rested from all his work." (5) And again in the passage above he says, "They shall never enter my rest." (6) It still remains that some will enter that rest, and those who formerly had the gospel preached to them did not go in, because of their disobedience."

By faith, Moses kept the Passover. By faith, they passed through the Red Sea. They never did doubt the essentials of their salvation. However, those who rejected the report of the godly spies did not enter into the promise land, the Millennial Reign.

Five Crowns

I found something very interesting as I studied the crowns that will be handed out at the Judgement Seat of Christ. It seems that there will be those who only receive one of the five crowns. In fact, I think that will probably be the majority. Jesus is the only one I see in the scriptures who receives all five of the crowns. Crown him with many crowns is more than just a favorite song of dentists. I'm wondering if qualifying for one of the crowns is what qualifies us for the rapture. Rather than thinking that we must excel in all of these qualifications, it may be that focusing on one of them will be sufficient.

There are five crowns that will be handed out at the Judgement Seat of Christ. What I want to do now is compare the five crowns to the five qualifiers of the overcomer.

The Crown of Incorruption

1 Corinthians 9:24-25 "Know ye not that they which run in a race run all, but one receiveth the prize? So run, that ye may obtain. (25) And every man that striveth for the mastery is temperate in all things. Now

they do it to obtain a corruptible crown; but we an incorruptible."

The crown of incorruption is attained by faith. One of the five qualifications for living an overcoming life is to live by faith. When Jesus comes back, will he find faith on the earth? Corruption comes from unbelief. The book of Romans says anything that does not come from faith is sin. All the corruption of the world comes from sin. The incorruptible crown is attained through faith.

The Crown of Life

James 1:12 "Blessed is the man who perseveres under trial, because when he has stood the test, he will receive the crown of life that God has promised to those who love him."

To persevere under trial; to resist temptation; even to die as a martyr all relate to being Spirit-filled. If we go back to the wilderness wandering account, we see something very interesting.

Numbers 14:6-8 "Joshua son of Nun and Caleb son of Jephunneh, who were among those who had explored the land, tore their clothes (7) and said to the entire Israelite assembly, "The land we passed through and explored is exceedingly good."

Now look at verse 10:

Numbers 14:10 "But the whole assembly talked about stoning them."

81

The only real difference between the overcomer and the one overcome, is his Spirit. The Spirit-filled man has a whole different perspective on life. He lives by faith. He sees what God sees. He doesn't see defeat.

Numbers 14:24-25 "But because my servant Caleb has a different Spirit and follows me wholeheartedly, I will bring him into the land he went to, and his descendants will inherit it."

In the parable of the ten virgins, the difference between the foolish and the wise was their Spirit.

Matthew 25:8 "The foolish ones said to the wise, `Give us some of your oil; our lamps are going out.'"

The lamp of the wise was filled with oil; the lamp of the foolish was not.

The Crown of Righteousness

2 Timothy 4:8 "Now there is in store for me the crown of righteousness, which the Lord, the righteous Judge, will award to me on that day-and not only to me, but also to all who have longed for his appearing."

The crown of righteousness goes to those who love His appearing. One of the five qualififiers of the overcomer is that he must be looking for Christ. The thought behind that is those who do not look for Him will not see Him. Longing for His appearing prompts us to perform acts of kindness, acts of mercy and compassion. If we live in anticipation of His return, we will do what we can to store up treasures in heaven.

The Crown of Rejoicing

1 Thessalonians 2:19 "For what is our hope, or joy, or crown of rejoicing? Are not even ye in the presence of our Lord Jesus Christ at his coming?" KJV

This crown relates to our work for Jesus. One of the qualifications for the rapture is that you must be a working Christian in the service of the Lord. The idea behind any thing we do for Jesus is the salvation of mankind. It doesn't matter if all you do is clean the Church – if you do it, as unto the Lord, then it all comes back to the overall mission of the Church. Those who work for the Lord will one day be able to rejoice in those whose lives were affected by their labors.

Can you imagine that? One day we will see the full fruit of our labors. Apparently, we will be able to rejoice along with Jesus over their lives.

The Crown of Glory

1 Peter 5:1-4 1 "To the elders among you, I appeal as a fellow elder, a witness of Christ's sufferings and one who also will share in the glory to be revealed: (2) Be shepherds of God's flock that is under your care, serving as overseers-not because you must, but because you are willing, as God wants you to be; not greedy for money,

but eager to serve; (3) not lording it over those entrusted to you, but being examples to the flock. (4) And when the Chief Shepherd appears, you will receive the crown of glory that will never fade away."

This is the crown for church leaders. To think that there is a special crown for those who lead God's flock should make every under-shepherd take a more serious look at what they do. The qualification that matches up with this is the one of purity. The first qualification we looked at was the one that says we must live a purified life. One of the verses associated with this is Titus 2:12:

"It teaches us to say "No" to ungodliness and worldly passions, and to live self-controlled, upright and godly lives in this present age."

This is not only descriptive of someone with a pure heart – it must also be the heart of God's shepherds. The pure in heart see God, or we could say, the pure in heart see what God's sees. When we see from God's perspective we go about his work with more diligence and passion.

So, these are the crowns - the crown of incorruption; the crown of rejoicing; the crown of glory; the crown of righteousness; and the crown of life. Here is the big question? Do you feel you qualify for one of these? Jesus is probably the only one who will receive all five of these crowns. Do you see yourself in this picture? If you cannot see yourself on this list at all, you need to ask yourself what it is you are doing for the Kingdom.

The value of these crowns is based on what they imply rather than for what they are. Satan is not trying to steal the actual physical crown as much as he is out to thwart our efforts to gain one of these crowns. Whoever earns a crown will simultaneously bring glory to Christ. We don't seek the crown for the sake of self-glory but rather to glorify Christ.

2 John 8, "Watch out that you do not lose what you have worked for, but that you may be rewarded fully."

Someone once said, *"What would it be like to see God's original draft of what our life was to be like, if only we would have fully obeyed."* Do you know what? We have a God of mercy. The whole nature of warnings comes from God's desire to do good to us. The Bible says that God will restore what the locust has eaten. That means, even if you feel that most of your life has been wasted; God can still bring good out of it. He is a God of the second, third, fourth, fifth, 490th chance. He forgives and forgives and forgives. He forgives and forgets and then forgets that He forgave.

Earlier, I said that the difference between the overcomer and the one who has been overcome is their

Spirit. An overcomer has a right Spirit. He is not necessarily a perfect man. We would proabably have to say that King David was an overcomer. Even though he had many setbacks, God said he was a man after His own heart. The overcomer does not give up: he continually picks himself up from his mistake, asks for forgiveness, and continues to move toward God. Always move toward God. Don't allow a struggle or a particular sin to keep you from going after God. God forgives!

Part Two

Random Stuff About the End Times

Chapter Ten

Daniel's Seventy Weeks

Daniel 9:20-27 "While I was speaking and praying, confessing my sin and the sin of my people Israel and making my request to the LORD my God for his holy hill- (21) while I was still in prayer, Gabriel, the man I had seen in the earlier vision, came to me in swift flight about the time of the evening sacrifice. (22) He instructed me and said to me, "Daniel, I have now come to give you insight and understanding. (23) As soon as you began to pray, an answer was given, which I have come to tell you, for you are highly esteemed. Therefore, consider the message and understand the vision: (24) "Seventy 'sevens' are decreed for your people and your holy city to finish transgression, to put an end to sin, to atone for wickedness, to bring in everlasting righteousness, to seal up vision and prophecy and to anoint the most holy. (25) "Know and understand this: From the issuing of the decree to restore and rebuild Jerusalem until the Anointed One, the ruler, comes, there will be seven 'sevens,' and sixty-two 'sevens.' It will be rebuilt with streets and a trench, but in times of trouble. (26) After the sixty-two 'sevens,' the Anointed One will be cut off and will have nothing. The people of the ruler who will come will destroy the city and the sanctuary. The end will come like a flood: War will continue until the end, and desolations have been decreed."

The two words in verse 24, **"Seventy Sevens,"** is our first clue in unraveling this prophecy. Some of the other translations say, "Seventy weeks." In either case, it simply means "seven." It's the   Hebrew word *"shabuwa"* which can mean a period of seven days, weeks, or years. What we understand from this prophecy is that this literally means seventy seven-year periods of time or 490 years.

The reason we are quite sure that it means 490 years is because of the prophecy, which Daniel detailed in the above verses. The prophecy begins with Daniel stating that once the decree goes out to start the rebuilding of Jerusalem, from that time the clock starts ticking. The way we interpret most prophecies is by looking backward at them. At the time this prophecy was given there was probably no way to understand it at all, however, with the passing of time we can look back at what was prophesied and compare that to the events it relates to.

Daniel 9:25, "Know and understand this: From the issuing of the decree to restore and rebuild Jerusalem until the Anointed One, the ruler, comes, there will be seven 'sevens,' and sixty-two 'sevens.' It will be rebuilt with streets and a trench, but in times of trouble. (26) After the sixty-two 'sevens,' the Anointed One will be cut off."

First of all he says that there will be seven sevens, which would mean 49 years, (7 X 7 = 49). Then he says there will also be sixty-two sevens which adds up to 434 years, (62 X 7 = 434). These two segments of time add up

89

to 69 weeks or 483 years. That means there is still one week or seven years of the prophecy to be fulfilled. Let's look at the first 49 years.

Nehemiah 2:17-18 "Then I said to them, "You see the trouble we are in: Jerusalem lies in ruins, and its gates have been burned with fire. Come, let us rebuild the wall of Jerusalem, and we will no longer be in disgrace." (18) I also told them about the gracious hand of my God upon me and what the king had said to me. They replied, "Let us start rebuilding." So they began this good work."

This is the decree referred to in verse 25 of Daniel 9. The reason we know that this is the decree Daniel referred to is because from the time of this decree to the end of the Old Testament was a period of 49 years or seven sevens. That is the first 'seven sevens,' or 49 years, He spoke of in Daniel 9:25. Then it says there will be a period of time lasting sixty-two sevens, or 434 years, lasting until the Anointed one gets cut off, referring to the death of Christ.

When the Old Testament ended there was a period of time called the "dark ages," which lasted 400 years. The birth of Christ ended the dark ages and brought us into the New Testament era. History shows us that Jesus lived 33 or 34 years. So, if we add up the 400 years of the dark ages and the 34 years of Christ's life until the anointed one was cut off (crucified), we have a period of 434 years or sixty-two sevens. That means we have fulfilled 69 of the 70 weeks so far and we are waiting for the last week, or seven-year period of time, to begin what we call the Tribulation period.

Daniel 9:27 "He will confirm a covenant with many for one 'seven.' In the middle of the 'seven' he will put an end to sacrifice and offering. And on a wing [of the temple] he will set up an abomination that causes desolation, until the end that is decreed is poured out on him."

He will confirm a peace covenant with Israel for one seven, or one-week of years. We can see this unfolding right before our eyes. The world is going to continually come against Israel, and as long as America is Israel's ally, we will continually be in the midst of the fray. The antichrist will eventually come on the scene as one with all the answers. He will bring the warring of the nations to a halt. He will come initially as a false prince of peace, as a puesdo Christ. The capstone of his work will be that of signing a peace accord with Israel. When that happens, we will be in the beginning of the Tribulation period. At any time then we can expect the first rapture of the Church to take the overcomers. This is the final week of seven years, which will fulfill Daniel's prophecy.

So we know that the Tribulation is the final "seven" of this prophecy. Just think of the accuracy of Daniel's prophecy. Almost five hundred years before Christ was born, he predicted His death. We have no reason to believe

91

that the rest of this prophecy will not be fulfilled. We are waiting for the final week or the seven-year period of the Tribulation to begin. The life we are living right now determines which rapture we go in.

Chapter Eleven

Nuclear War

The early Church and the apostles preached about the soon return of Christ so this subject is an old as the Church itself. When I was saved in 1973, there was much talk about the rapture. It had not been that long since the 1967 six-day war, when Israel regained control of Jerusalem. I remember an evangelist who came to our Church and stated that there was no possible way that the world could go beyond 1975. There was a great assumption that Israel would take over the shrine that the Muslims now control and rebuild the temple. Obvioulsy, he missed it by a few years.

The temple must be rebuilt in order for the antichrist to commit the abomination of desolation, when he sits on the throne and declares himself to be God. Today many Jews still go to the western wall, or wailing wall, to pray for the return of the temple to the Jewish people.

Consider this: Noah worked for 120 years building the Ark with the message that a flood in the form of God's judgment was going to come upon the earth. For 120 years he preached that message. The partially built ark was the continual testimony of pending judgment. For 120 years the people heard the warning. How many of us have lived 120 years? And yet some people today dismiss the possibility of Christ's soon return because they have heard it for 50 years and it hasn't happened yet. We are probably a lot more like the people of Noah's day than we want to admit.

So let's look at some issues regarding the return of Christ. One of the things we see in the scriptures is that every time God did something significant He gave a warning to His children. For 120 years Noah preached about the judgment that would come while he constructed the Ark on dry ground, when suddenly, seven days before the flood God warned Him. Lot knew the day before Sodom was to be destroyed. God does set signs in the sky that we can read.

I'm afraid the Church used to preach about the rapture so frequently, we learnd to tune it out and we became quite skeptical about the subject. Some even believe we are living in the Millennial Reign of Christ today. However, I don't think that's possible because of the event I'm about to describe. When it comes to the Tribulation period it would have been impossible for it to take place prior to the last century. I once heard a teaching by Rev. James Singleton about how the Bible clearly describes a nuclear war during the Tribulation.

In the 1970"'s there was an article in the National Gergraphic magazine, of a time when our Airfore detonated a hydrogen bomb in the air. There is what's called the Van Allen belts around the earth's atmosphere. The Van Allen belts are a collection of charged particles, trapped by Earth's magnetic field. They can wax and wane in response to incoming energy from the sun. The belt's presence was confirmed by the Explorer I on January 31, 1958, under Doctor James van Allen for whom the belt was named.

Before they could detonate it, they had to make sure it was at an altitude to where the mushroom from the bomb would not get caught-up into the Van Allen belt, because that would have circulated radiation around the earth for an undetermined amount of time. If that had happened the Air Force said, the sun would have been blotted out; it would have been dark in the midst of daytime, and at night the moon would have looked like red human blood.

The Tribulation period is not going to be a nice time on earth. Many of the things we are worried about today concerning nuclear war effects are going to happen during this time.

Revelation 6:9-14 "When he opened the fifth seal, I saw under the altar the souls of those who had been slain because of the word of God and the testimony they had maintained. (10) They called out in a loud voice, "How long, Sovereign Lord, holy and true, until you

judge the inhabitants of the earth and avenge our blood?" (11) Then each of them was given a white robe, and they were told to wait a little longer, until the full number of their fellow servants, their brothers and sisters, were killed just as they had been. (12) I watched as he opened the sixth seal. There was a great earthquake. The sun turned black like sackcloth made of goat hair, the whole moon turned blood red, (13) and the stars in the sky fell to earth, as figs drop from a fig tree when shaken by a strong wind. (14) The heavens receded like a scroll being rolled up, and every mountain and island was removed from its place."

Our timeline is the Tribulation period, when the sun will not shine in the middle of the day because of a nuclear holocaust, and the moon will be red like blood. When they detonated the hydrogen bomb, the Navy was in the Pacific Ocean to observe the event. When the plane was about to drop the bomb, something malfunctioned and the bomb went off much sooner than it was supposed to. Because of that, it missed the Van Allen belt by a very small margin. However the Navy men who were observing this from the ship found themselves running for cover, because 40 and 50 pound chunks of ice were falling out of the sky. Revelation 6:13 says. **"And the stars in the sky fell to earth."**

We must keep in mind that John the Revelator, who had his vision on the Island of Patmos, would have had no idea what a hydrogen bomb was or a nuclear war. I would imagine that 40 and 50 pound chunks of ice falling from a darkened sky, would look like stars falling. It seems the Revelator witnessed, in the Spirit, a nuclear war in the midst of the Tribulation period.

Chapter Twelve

The Millennial Reign

(Much of the material in the next two chapters is taken from David Guzik's Commentaries on the Bible.)

Before we can get into the details of the Thousand Year Reign of Christ, we have to determine where the old enemy is during this time. In Revelation 20 we find out Satan is bound almost the entire time of Christ's reign on earth.

Revelation 20:1-3 "And I saw an angel coming down out of heaven, having the key to the Abyss and holding in his hand a great chain. (2) He seized the dragon, that ancient serpent, who is the devil, or Satan, and bound him for a thousand years. (3) He threw him into the Abyss, and locked and sealed it over him, to keep him from deceiving the nations anymore until the thousand years were ended. After that, he must be set free for a short time."

He is not bound by Jesus Himself, nor is it Michael or Gabriel or any other high-ranking angel. The angel that will subdue Satan is anonymouns. Can you imagine this scenario in hell? Satan gets thrown down there and all the hordes of hell gather around him and in hushed tones they whisper to each other, *"Wow, it's Satan himself."*

With all the courage Demon can muster he asks, *"Who threw you down here? Was it God?"*

Satan says, *"No."*

Demon asks, *"Was it Jesus?"*

Satan fires back, *"No it wasn't Jesus!"*

"It must have been Michael or Gabriel then," Demon countered.

"No, it wasn't. I think it was an angel named Fred. Yes, Fred the angel did this to me." Satan admitted.

"The final importance of Satan is perhaps indicated in the fact that it is not the Father who deals with him, nor the Christ but only an unnamed angel," (Morris)

These verses in Revelation 20 are a dramatic declaration that Satan is *not* God's opposite or equal. He is in opposition to God, but not his opposite in any way. Satan is imprisoned for a thousand years. It's kind of satisfying to note that Satan tried to imprison Jesus in a tomb, but couldn't. Here God has no problem restraining Satan, and this incarceration is not for punishment, but restraint. By implication, his demonic hordes are also imprisoned.

Some people might ask, *"What kind of chain can hold the devil?"* We don't know, but God can fashion a chain for that exact purpose. We know that right now there are demonic Spirits who are imprisoned and chained (Jude 6). If God can chain them now, He can chain Satan for a thousand years. He is bound till the thousand years are completed, then he is loosed for a very short period of time.

This thousand-year period is know as the Millennium or the Millennial Reign of Christ or simply the thousand years. It will last from the time of the second coming of Christ at the battle of Armageddon until the creation of the New Heaven and New Earth. However, just prior to the actual start of the Millennium, there must be the judgment of the nations.

Matthew 25:31-34 "When the Son of Man comes in his glory, and all the angels with him, he will sit on his glorious throne. (32) All the nations will be gathered before him, and he will separate the people one from another as a shepherd separates the sheep from the goats. (33) He will put the sheep on his right and the goats on his left. (34) "Then the King will say to those on his right, 'Come, you who are blessed by my Father; take your inheritance, the kingdom prepared for you since the creation of the world."

When Jesus sits upon the throne of His glory, it marks the coming of the Son of Man at the end of the Great Tribulation to usher in the Millenniun. Before Him shall be gathererd all the nations of the world as He separates the sheep from the goats.

This judgment scene must be distinguished from that of Revelation 20 (Great White Throne Judgment), which comes after the resurrection of the wicked at the close of the Millennium. Here, the nations refer to the persons living on earth when Christ returns. Such a judgment of living men at the time of Christ's glorious coming is foretold:

Joel 3:1-2 "In those days and at that time, when I restore the fortunes of Judah and Jerusalem, (2) I will gather all nations and bring them down to the Valley of Jehoshaphat. There I will put them on trial for what they did to my inheritance, my people Israel, because they scattered my people among the nations and divided up my land."

It will result in a separation into two groups, with the group compared to sheep placed at Christ's right hand, the position of honor and blessing. The unrighteous, the goats, go away to eternal punishment, where they stay until the Great White Throne Judgment (more about that later).

Who will be on the earth in the Millennium? Even after the rapture and the vast judgments of the Great Tribulation, there will be many people left on earth. Not all men die during the Tribulation; many of them will pass from one dispensation to the next in the same way many people living during the Old Testament age suddenly found themselves living during the New Testament age upon the birth of Christ.

This is what we know of the Millennium from other passages of Scripture. During this time Israel will be the "superpower" of the world. It will be the leading nation in all the earth, and the center of Israel will be *the mountain of the Lord's house* – the temple mount, which will be the "capital" of the government of the Messiah. All nations shall flow to this "capital" of the government of Jesus (Isaiah 2:1-3).

The citizens of earth will acknowledge and submit to the Lordship of Jesus. It will be a time of perfectly administrated, and enforced righteousness, on this earth. There will still be conflicts between individuals, but the Messiah and those who reign with Him (the overcomers), will justly and decisively resolve them, (Isaiah 2:1-5).

Let's let the Word of God itself describe the Millennial kingdom:

Isaiah 65:17-25 "See, I will create new heavens and a new earth. The former things will not be remembered, nor will they come to mind. (18) But be glad and rejoice forever in what I will create, for I will create Jerusalem to be a delight and its people a joy. (19) I will rejoice over Jerusalem and take delight in my people; the sound of weeping and of crying will be heard in it no more. (20) "Never again will there be in it an infant who lives but a few days, or an old man who does not live out his years; the one who dies at a hundred will be thought a mere child; the one who fails to reach a hundred will be considered accursed. (21) They will build houses and dwell in them; they will plant vineyards and eat their fruit. (22) No longer will they build houses and others live

in them, or plant and others eat. For as the days of tree, so will be the days of my people; my chosen ones will long enjoy the work of their hands. (23) They will not labor in vain, nor will they bear children doomed to misfortune; for they will be a people blessed by the Lord, they and their descendants with them. (24) Before they call I will answer; while they are still speaking I will hear. (25) The wolf and the lamb will feed together, and the lion will eat straw like the ox, and dust will be the serpent's food. They will neither harm nor destroy on all my holy mountain," says the Lord.

You really cannot get a better description of this time than what Isaiah prophesied. Some people think these verses pertain to our eternal dwelling place, rather than the Millennial reign. The problem with that is found in verse 20 which talks about people dying. There will be no death once we finally reach our eternal home.

It's interesting to note that it isn't merely the reign of the Messiah alone that will change the heart of man during this era, as we shall see in the final rebellion. Citizens of earth will still need to trust in Jesus and His work on their behalf for their personal salvation during the Millennium. But war and armed conflict will not be tolerated.

During the Millennium, the way animals relate to each other and to humans will be transformed. A little child will be safe and able to lead a wolf, a leopard, a young lion, or a bear. Even the danger of predators, like cobras and vipers, will be gone (Isaiah 11:6-9).

In Genesis 9:2-3, the Lord gave Noah and all mankind after him permission to eat meat. At the same time, the Lord put the *dread* of man in animals, so they would not be effortless prey for humans. Now, in the reign of the Messiah, that is reversed. For this reason, many think that in the reign of the Messiah, the Millennial humans,will return to being vegetarians, as it seems they were before Genesis 9.

During the Millennium, saints (the overcomers) in their resurrected state will be given responsibilities in the Millennial Earth according to their faithful service (Luke 19:11-27; Revelation 2:26-28, 3:12,22, 20:4-6; 1 Corinthians 6:2-3).

The Millennium is a literal thousand years. God has an important work to accomplish during this time. It will demonstrate Jesus' victory and worthiness to rule the nations. It's also important because it will reveal the depth, of man's rebellious natue in a perfect environment, (Revelaiton 20:11-15). Afer the thousand years are finished, there is another rebellion against God. This revolt will display the eternal depravity of Satan, who continues his evil as soon as he is released from his incarceration.

The Overcomers

Now let's look at those who will be reigning with Christ during this time.

Revelation 20:4 "And I saw thrones, and they sat upon them, and judgment was given to them. And I saw the souls of those who had been beheaded because of the testimony of Jesus and because of the word of God, and those who had not worshiped the beast or his image, and had not received the mark upon their forehead and upon their hand; and they came to life and reigned with Christ for a thousand years."

Revelation 2:26 "To the one who is victorious and does my will to the end, I will give authority over the nations."

These two portions of scripture show us two groups of saints who rule with Christ - the martyrs, as stated in Revelation 20, and the overcomers, as stated in Matthew 25 and various other places. These saints reign with Jesus for the same period of time that Satan is bound (a thousand years). They administrate the kingdom of Jesus Christ over the earth, reigning over those who pass from the earth of the Great Tribulation to the earth of the Millennium.

Those who rule and reign with Christ have finished their course regarding their salvation. Once the corruptible puts on the incorruptible, they will no longer be subject to the whims of the flesh as they had been during their days on earth. First Corthinans 15 talks about how we will be changed in the twinkling of an eye at the time of the rapture.

1 Corinthians 15:52-54 "In a flash, in the twinkling of an eye, at the last trumpet. For the trumpet will sound, the deadwill be raised imperishable, and we will be changed. (53) For the perishable must clothe itself with the imperishable, and the mortal with immortality. (54) When the perishable has been clothed with the imperishable, and the mortal with immortality, then the saying that is written will come true: "Death has been swallowed up in victory."

When Christ was raised from the dead and walked the earth before His resurrection, His former corriptible body had become His new incorruptible body. Two different times Jesus walked through a closed door in the gospel of John. In chapter 20 verses 19 & 26, we see Jesus suddenluy appearing in a room where the disciples were, though an emphasis is made that the door was shut. Because of this it's assumed that our resurrected bodies will have the same capabalities. We will not be subject to the same laws of physics that we are today.

In the very next chapter of John we see Jesus dining on fish with the disciples. Even though He was in his resurrected body He still had the ability to eat solid food, but most comentators do not feel we will have the need for it - though it will be possible.

Revelation 20:6 "Blessed and holy are those who share in the first resurrection. The second death has no power over them, but they will be priests of God and of Christ and will reign with him for a thousand years."

Four different times the book of Revelation talks of the second death. That is a reference to those who are being judged at the Great White Throne Judgment. For those who have gone to heaven, or were raptured in Christ, the second death does not apply. Therefore, the redeemed have no need to worry about the kind of things we worry about today. Our judgment took place on the cross. Jesus paid that price for us. We need not worry about backsliding or even being sujbect to temptation during this time.

The Final Battle

There is one last rebellion at the very end of the Millennium.

Revelation 20:7-8 "And when the thousand years are completed, Satan will be released from his prison, (8) and will come out to deceive the nations which are in the four corners of the earth, Gog and Magog, to gather them together for the war; the number of them is like the sand of the seashore."

It's quite amazing that there is still a rebellious Spirit in the hearts of so many. If Jesus has reigned so wonderfully for a thousand years, then why will the earth rebel? They will do it, and God will allow it, as a final demonstration of man's rebellion and depravity. *Outward* conformity to Jesus' rule will be required during His reign, but, seemingly, an inward embrace of His Lordship will still be up to the individual. In this we see more of the important reason God has for the Millennial Kingdom and allowing this final rebellion. In all of human history, man has wanted to blame his sinful condition on his *environment* - "*Of course, I turned out the way I did. Did you see the family I came from? Did you see the neighborhood I grew up in?*" In the Millennial Kingdom, God will give mankind a thousand years of a perfect environment - with no Satan, no crime, no violence, no evil, or any other social pathology. But at the end of the thousand years, man will still rebel against God at his first opportunity. This will powerfully demonstrate that the problem is in *us*, not only in our environment.

Who will these rebels be? They will come from those who survive the Great Tribulation and enter into the Millennial Kingdom, and from their descendants. Life will go on much like it does today with marriage; births, deaths, and so forth. Many will turn to Christ during this time – but many will not.

This Battle Ends Before it Begins

Revelation 20:9-10 "And they came up on the broad plain of the earth and surrounded the camp of the saints and the beloved city, and fire came down from heaven and devoured them. (10) And the devil who deceived them was thrown into the lake of fire and brimstone, where the beast and the false prophet are also; and they will be tormented day and night forever and ever."

We don't really know if they surround the glorified saints, who reign with Jesus, or earth-inhabitants, who come to faith in Jesus during the Millennium. Either way, the strategy of this vast Satanic army is clear: to destroy God's people, and the "headquarters" or "capital city" of His administration, Jerusalem (the beloved city). Regardless of all of that, this battle is over in a heart-beat.

Mere man cannot hope to actually battle against God, though he has tried many times. In 2 Kings 19, one death angel put to death 185,000 men. That was just one angel. Can you imagine what God himself can accomplish with His mere breath? Don't believe the lie. Live for Jesus!

Judgment at the Great White Throne

Revelation 20:11 "And I saw a great white throne and Him who sat upon it, from whose presence earth and heaven fled away, and no place was found for them."

After the final battle, we come to the Great White Throne Judgment. This throne is great in status, power and authority; it's white in purity and holiness; and a throne in kingly sovereignty. Jesus sits on this throne.

This is such an awsome scene that the presence of earth and heaven flee away. There is absolutely no hiding from this throne. No one can escape the judgment that it represents. This is more than we can imagine – it's almost as though this throne encompasses the entire existence. It's as though this will be all anyone can see. There will not be a mountainous background with a bright blue sky – all there will be is the Great White Throne. Christians will never appear before this great white throne to be judged. This is not for those of us who were judged at Calvary.

Revelation 20:12 "And I saw the dead, the great and the small, standing before the throne, and books were opened; and another book was opened, which is the book of life; and the dead were judged from the things which were written in the books, according to their deeds. "

Keep in mind this is not a trial, trying to determine what the facts are. The facts are in; here is the sentencing of someone already condemned. "Their standing posture means that they are now about to be sentenced," (Walvoord).

Because this is not a trial, but a sentencing, there is nothing for those who stand before the throne to say. Many think they will "tell God a thing or two" at the final judgment. Of course, there will be no criticism of God on that day.

Revelation 20:13 "And the sea gave up the dead which were in it, and death and Hades gave up the dead which were in them; and they were judged, every one of them according to their deeds."

If people are not listed in the Book of Life, then each one is judged according to his works. Those who refused to come to God by faith will, by default, be judged (and condemned) by their works.

Matthew 12:35-37 35 "A good man out of the good treasure of the heart bringeth forth good things: and an evil man out of the evil treasure bringeth forth evil things. (36) But I say unto you, That every idle word that men shall speak, they shall give account thereof in the day of judgment. (37) For by thy words thou shalt be justified, and by thy words thou shalt be condemned." KJV

"The issue is not salvation by works, but works as the irrefutable evidence of a man's actual relationship with God." (Mounce)

Revelation 20:14 "Then death and Hades were thrown into the lake of fire. The lake of fire is the second death. (15) Anyone whose name was not found written in the book of life was thrown into the lake of fire."

The last echoes of sin are now eliminated. Death is the result of sin, and it is gone. Hades is the result of death,

111

and it is gone. The last vestiges of sin's unlawful domination are done away with.

This is the second death: "As there is a second and higher life, so there is also a second and deeper death. And as after that life there is no more death, so after that death there is no more life" (Alford)

"The devil and the damned have punishment without pity, misery without mercy, sorrow without succor, crying without comfort, mischief without measure, torments without end and past imagination." (Trapp)

The end is not good for those whose names were not found in the Lamb's Book of Life. There is not a more critical decision we can make than to decide to surrender our wills to the will of Jesus.

Chapter Thirteen

New Heaven and New Earth

Death and Hades are cast into the lake of fire

Revelation 21:1 "And I saw a new heaven and a new earth; for the first heaven and the first earth passed away, and there is no longer any sea."

Revelation chapter 21 begins a new section of the Book of Revelation. Here is how the book breaks down:

Jesus, the Lord of the Churches (Revelation 1:1 to 3:22)
Jesus, the Lion over the nations (Revelation 4:1 to 20:15)
Jesus, the Lamb among believers (Revelation 21:1 - 22:21)

The idea of a new earth, with a new atmosphere and sky, is a familiar theme in the scriptures. Many of the prophets, in both the Old and New Testaments spoke to this new heaven and new earth.

It's worth remembering that the new heaven referred to doesn't mean the heaven where God is enthroned. The Bible uses the word heaven in three senses.

The first heaven is the earth's atmosphere, the "blue sky." The second heaven is outer space, the "night sky." The third heaven is the place where God lives in glory.

When the scriptures speak of a new heaven, they mean a new "blue sky" and a new "night sky," not a new heaven where God dwells.

The ancient Greek word translated new here (*kaine*) means "new in character, 'fresh'." It doesn't mean "recent" or "new in time." *"In this chapter we see that the history of time is finished; the history of eternity is about to begin."* (Barnhouse)

The New Jerusalem Descends from Heaven

Revelation 21:2-4 "And I saw the holy city, new Jerusalem, coming down out of heaven from God, made ready as a bride adorned for her husband. (3) And I heard a loud voice from the throne, saying, "Behold, the tabernacle of God is among men, and He shall dwell among them, and they shall be His people, and God Himself shall be among them, (4) and He shall wipe away every tear from their eyes; and there shall no longer be any death; there shall no longer be any mourning, or crying, or pain; the first things have passed away. "

The terms "holy" and "new" distinguish the city. Because it is holy and new, it is different from any earthly city. The name Jerusalem gives it continuity with earth, especially with the place of our redemption.

It is significant that this glorious dwelling place of God and His people is described as the holy city. Cities are places where there are many people, and people interact with each other. This isn't isolation, but a perfect community of the people of God.

Man has never known a community unmarred by sin. Adam and Eve only knew a limited community, and community in a larger context only came long after the Fall. Here, in the New Jerusalem, we have something totally unique: a sinless, pure, community of righteousness, a holy city.

This is the greatest glory of heaven, and the ultimate restoration of what was lost in the Fall. I do not think the glory of Eden was in it's beautiful surroundings, but its glory lay in this, that the 'Lord God walked in the garden in the cool of the day.' Here was Adam's highest privilege - that he had companionship with the Most High.

The New Jerusalem is distinguished by what it does not have - no tears, no sorrow, no death or pain. no temple, no sacrifice, no sun, no moon, no darkness, no sin, and no abomination.

God will wipe away every tear from their eyes. It appears that there will be no memory of the struggles of this life or of those we loved who did not surrender their lives to Christ. Every tear will be wiped away, every memory, every heartache, and every failure will no longer be remembered.

Revelation 21:5 "He who was seated on the throne said, "I am making everything new!" Then he said, "Write this down, for these words are trustworthy and true."

When God finally completes this work of making all things new, they will stay new. "Presumably this means not only that everything will be made new, but also that everything will stay then new. The entropy law will be 'repealed.' Nothing will wear out or decay, and no one will age or atrophy anymore." (H. Morris)

Before the Fall

The traditional thought is that before the fall man reflected the image of God perfectly – however, I wonder if that is not quite the case. If they had reflected the image of God perfectly in every way, would they have sinned? I wonder if it might be better to say that what God created was perfect, but man's free will took advantage of the goodness of God and rebelled against him.

Although today each person is still created in the image of God, that image continues to be veiled due to the sinfulness of humanity. Prior to the fall, Adam and Eve walked with God and enjoyed perfect fellowship with him.

After the Fall

After the fall, it's a different story. The effects of this first sin upon our first parents were shame; a sense of degradation and pollution; dread of the displeasure of God; a sense of guilt, with the consequent desire to hide from His presence. These effects were unavoidable. They prove the loss not only of innocence, but of original righteousness, and, with it, of the favor and fellowship of God.

Even Satan was created as a perfect being, though he was not a human being.

Ezekiel 28:12-13 "You were the seal of perfection, full of wisdom and perfect in beauty. (13) You were in Eden, the garden of God."

He was created as a flawless angelic being.

Ezekiel 28:14 "You were anointed as a guardian cherub."

But in verse 15 it says:

Ezekiel 28:15 You were blameless in your ways from the day you were created till wickedness was found in you.

The same could be said of Adam and Eve. They were blameless in their ways until wickedness was found in them. When Adam sinned, the state to which he was reduced by his disobedience, so far as his individual condition was

117

concerned, was equivalent to that of the fallen angels. He was entirely and absolutely ruined.

Why God Allowed the Fall

So the question is why did God allow the Fall? Why didn't he just keep Adam from being tempted? Why did God allow evil in the first place?

John 9:2-3 "And his disciples asked him, "Rabbi, who sinned, this man or his parents, that he was born blind?" (3) Jesus answered, "It was not that this man sinned, or his parents, but that the works of God might be displayed in him."

There is a deep and instructive principle in these words. I believe Jesus' words throw light on that great question as to why did God allow the origin of evil. When Jesus answered His disciples and said, the man's blindness is nothing more than a stage for the works of God to be displayed, He revealed something quite critical. God thought it fit to allow evil to exist in order that He may have a platform for showing His mercy, grace, and compassion. If man had never fallen, or in this case, if this man had not been born blind, there would have been no opportunity of showing divine mercy. But by permitting this man's blindness, mysterious as it seems, God's works of grace, mercy, and wisdom in saving sinners is wonderfully manifested to all

His creatures. The redeeming of the Church is the means of "showing to principalities and powers the manifold wisdom of God." That's what Ephesians 3:10-11 is all about.

Ephesians 3:10-11 "His intent was that now, through the Church, the manifold wisdom of God should be made known to the rulers and authorities in the heavenly realms, (11) according to his eternal purpose that he accomplished in Christ Jesus our Lord."

Here's an interesting thought. God's intent was that now through the Church, through the redeemed, the wisdom of God would be made known to the rulers and authorities in the heavenly realms. We see later in the book of Ephesians that these rulers and authorities are the devil and his hordes.

Ephesians 6:12 "For our struggle is not against flesh and blood, but against the rulers, against the authorities, against the powers of this dark world and against the Spiritual forces of evil in the heavenly realms."

God's intent in allowing evil to exist was to show these powers and authorities, which rebelled against Him and have become our battle ground, that through the redemption of the Church, God has righted what the enemy wronged.

Think about this for a moment: we call Adam's sin original sin; it was in regard to man, however, the very first sin was Satan's rebellion against God. Some theologians believe that Satan existed in the garden with Adam and Eve before he fell from grace. We read that verse earlier from Ezekiel.

Ezekiel 28:12-13 "You were the seal of perfection, full of wisdom and perfect in beauty. (13) You were in Eden, the garden of God."

Some believe he might have been there for hundred's of years before God found unrighteousness in him. Keep in mind that Adam named all the animals before the fall. God said that he put Adam in the garden to work it and to keep it. We don't really know how long Adam and Eve were in the garden before they sinned. We don't even know how long Adam was there by himself before God created Eve. But the greater point I want to make is this: no one deceived Satan in the way Satan deceived Eve. The Bible says he was crafty and lied to Eve. However, when it comes to Satan, he flat out rebelled against God. No one tried to deceive him. He thought he could become like God. That is the craftiness he used against Eve, when he said to her in Genesis 3:5, **"When you eat of this fruit you will be like God."** Satan committed the original sin and then he deceived innocent man. However, I'm not attempting to excuse Adam's sin. God himself explicitly told him that he should not eat from the tree of knowledge of good and evil. So he chose to sin and paid a price for it.

Do you know how easy it would be to deceive an innocent person? First of all, innocence has no sense of deception, so it wouldn't even know it's being deceived. An evil person could easily deceive someone who is innocent. Do you know how easy it would be for anyone to tell a two year old lies about life? It would be simple. It's not that different from parents who refuse to teach their children about Jesus. If you are teaching them humanism, you are deceiving them about life.

Therefore, since Satan deceived man, but was not deceived himself, and openly rebelled against God, there has been no redemption offered to him and his fallen angels like there is to man. There is no evidence anywhere in the scriptures where God offers redemption to Satan and his gang of fallen angels. Man was deceived, but Satan knew what he was doing.

God, through the redemption of man, made known to these principalities and powers, who wage war against us, that in His manifold wisdom He has righted the wrong they put upon us. We need to praise God that he offers to us redemption through His Son. Without the Fall of Man, we would never have known anything of the Cross and the Gospel.

Redeemed or Innocent

Now we are going to pick up this verse again.

Rev 21:5-6 "And He who sits on the throne said, "Behold, I am making all things new." And He said, "Write, for these words are faithful and true."

When this verse stated, "**He who sat on the throne said,**" that is an authoritative announcement, coming from the throne of God itself. This is one of the few times in Revelation where we clearly see God speaking directly from His throne. And His words are: "**Behold, I make all things new.**" This statement is in the present tense, meaning; "**I am making everything new.**" This is the consummation of God's work of renewal and redemption.

Paul saw this transformation at work on this side of eternity:

2 Corinthians 4:16, 5:17 "Therefore we do not lose heart. Even though our outward man is perishing, yet the inward man is being renewed day by day . . .
Therefore, if anyone is in Christ, he is a new creation; old things have passed away; behold, all things have become new."

This is a brief glance at the thinking behind God's eternal plan, which was to allow sin and its destruction, in order to do a greater work of making all things new. At this point in His plan of the ages, the plan is complete. If you are in Christ, all things have been made new. Your old life has passed away and all things have become new to you.

Psalms 51:5 "Surely I was sinful at birth, sinful from the time my mother conceived me."

Because of Adam's sin all men are born in sin, however when we are born-again, the stain of original sin is removed and God makes us new. Why do you think a person's life changes so dramatically when they receive Christ as their Savior? It's because He literally brings them into a new life. It's the life of the redeemed. And it's almost as though he is rubbing it in Satan's face and saying, *"I have made new the very thing you corrupted, but you Satan, will be lost forever."*

We need to understand something about redemption - it is much better than innocence. Our instinct is to romantically consider innocence as man's perfect state; subsequently, we wish Adam had not sinned. Have you ever said something like that? Have you ever had the thought, *"I wish we were still in the Garden?"* I have. However, in that state of mind we fail to realize that **redeemed man is greater than innocent man in that we gain more in Jesus than we ever lost in Adam.** God's perfect state is one of redemption, not innocence. Innocence has no revelation of the mercy and grace of God. In innocence, Adam walked with God. In redemption, God dwells within man. Which is better? In the Old Testament, prior to the redemptive work of Jesus, the Holy Spirit was with men. But in the New Testament, because of what Jesus accomplished on the cross, the Holy Spirit can now dwell within man. Which is better?

The redeemed of the Lord are those who openly and willfully choose God over this world. The lost are those who openly and willfully choose the world over God. Those who are redeemed prove their love for the Lord. If a man had no free will, he might end up saved without even having an affinity for the Lord. He wouldn't care whether or not he served the Lord, because he would not have had a choice.

Freedom of choice is the beauty of every relationship. If there were no choice, there would be no attractiveness to marriage. If divorce were not an option, marriage would have very little merit. But because you can walk away, staying together is proof of your love. The same is true in our relationship with Jesus. Man fell because he willfully chose to sin; redemption comes to him when he willfully chooses to follow God. Man fell, yes, but God redeems. Praise Him!

The New Jerusalem, the Bride of Christ

Revelation 21:9 "And one of the seven angels who had the seven bowls full of the seven last plagues, came

and spoke with me, saying, "Come here, I shall show you the bride, the wife of the Lamb."

This heavenly city is literal. It is called the bride, the Lamb's wife because it is the place where all God's people are gathered.

Revelation 21:11-14 "Having the glory of God. Her brilliance was like a very costly stone, as a stone of crystal-clear jasper. (12) It had a great and high wall, with twelve gates, and at the gates twelve angels; and names were written on them, which are those of the twelve tribes of the sons of Israel. (13) There were three gates on the east and three gates on the north and three gates on the south and three gates on the west. (14) And the wall of the city had twelve foundation stones, and on them were the twelve names of the twelve apostles of the Lamb."

John the Revelator is awestruck by the glory of this city. She shares in the glory of God, and it is expressed in the radiant light that shines from her. There are twelve gates with names written on them, which are the names of the twelve tribes of the children of Israel. The wall of the city has twelve foundations, and on them are the names of the twelve Apostles of the Lamb.

When Revelation 21:11 said that this city has the glory of God within it, I was reminded of Ephesians 1:6, which says that we were adpoted to sonship, to the praise of His glory. The redeemed of the Lord are the glory of his grace. So when we think of the New Jerusalem having his glory we need to think of it as the Bride of Christ more so than just a phyical building.

One time, while in Africa, we drove through a village out in the bush. While taking in the sights, and sounds, and beauty of Africa, I suddenly noticed four poles holding up a thatched roof. There were no physical walls, just four poles, a roof, and a dirt floor. What caught my attention was a makeshift sign with a some words scribbled on it which read: *All to His Glory Church.*

In the western world our image of a church is a building, not so in Africa. In Africa the focus is on the people of God more than the building they meet in. The church is made up of people, the called out ones; buildings have nothing to do with it, and yet the building seems to be the measure of the success of the church.

It is precisely because of this particular mind-set that all we can think of when the bible talks of the New Jerusalem is a building. Though the bible describes it as having structure, we may not want to jump to conclusions as to what makes up the walls of the Bride of Christ.

Revelation 21:15-17 "The angel who talked with me had a measuring rod of gold to measure the city, its gates and its walls. (16) The city was laid out like a square, as long as it was wide. He measured the city with the rod and found it to be 12,000 stadia in length, and as

wide and high as it is long. (17) The angel measured the wall using human measurement, and it was 144 cubits thick."

How large is the city? That varies slightly depending on the version of the Bible. The ESV and NIV versions say it is 12,000 stadia in length and width - a stadia is 607 feet. This translates to 1,400 miles, which is what the NLT Bible says. However, the KJV and other versions say 12,000 furlongs, which equals 1,500 miles.

Regardless of whether the city is 1,400 miles or 1,500 miles in length and width it's big. It is shaped like a square at the base. This means the New Jerusalem is larger than India with nearly 2 million square miles. These measurements are meant to be literal, since they are described as man's measurements.

Even more astounding than the size of the base is the height, that is also at least 1,400 miles. This goes well beyond Earth's atmosphere and into space. If a building in the city is that high and has a generous 12 feet per story, the building would be over 600,000 stories! This is the same distance from Maine to Florida; the square footage would approximate the size of the Moon.

Henry Morris, guessing that there will have been 100 billion people in the human race, and that 20% of them will be saved, calculates that each person would have a "block" with about 75 acres each to "call his own."

Revelation 21:18-21 "The wall was made of jasper, and the city of pure gold, as pure as glass. (19) The foundations of the city walls were decorated with every kind of precious stone. The first foundation was jasper, the second sapphire, the third agate, the fourth emerald, (20) the fifth onyx, the sixth ruby, the seventh chrysolite, the eighth beryl, the ninth topaz, the tenth turquoise, the eleventh jacinth, and the twelfth amethyst. (21) The twelve gates were twelve pearls, each gate made of a single pearl. The great street of the city was of gold, as pure as transparent glass."

When we read of jasper and pure gold and all kinds of precious stones, we should take these as literal representations; they express realities of another world. We can gain a brief glimpse of what John saw, but we can't even begin to appreciate its fullness until we see it with our own eyes. The beauty of its structure is beyond our human comprehension. However, we must understand that this is the city whose architect and maker is God as **Hebrews 11:10** states: **"For he was looking forward to the city with foundations, whose architect and builder is God."** We should expect it to be beyond our comprehension.

John's use of material riches to describe the city "is his way of bringing out the very great value of what God has for His people," (Morris). If there is any Biblical reference point for this assortment of gemstones, it is probably the High Priest's breastplate (Exodus 28:15-21).

Consider what 1 Peter says about this house that God designed.

1 Peter 2:5 "You also, as living stones, are being built up as a Spiritual house for a holy priesthood, to offer up Spiritual sacrifices acceptable to God through Jesus Christ."

Not until we really think about the New Jerusalem would this verse make sense. We must keep in mind that God is the designer and, therefore, we cannot limit the imagination to what man has been able to accomplish. Though man has created some amazing things, mere man could never design a building where human beings make up the walls of the building. Peter said that we are living stones being built up as a Spiritual house. Could it be that we will make up the walls of the city and that will be our place of eternal dwelling? Could it be that while this city is called the New Jerusalem, it is also called the Bride of Christ, because the redeemed of the Lord actually become the essence of the city?

John 14:2 "In My Father's house (singular) are many dwelling places; if it were not so, I would have told you; for I go to prepare a place for you."

John said that the Father has one house with many dwelling places. God has one dwelling place and we will live in that house. People often talk about their eternal dwelling place as a mansion on a hilltop, or a cabin on a lake, but when you really think about it, wouldn't you really rather live in our Father's house?

When I was younger and I would go home for Christmas, there was something very special about being in my parents home. It just felt right. I would not have wanted to travel to my home town for a special time and then just stay in a hotel when my parents had a room for me. Not only has Jesus prepared a room for us in his fathers house, it might just be that we make up the very walls of the house ourselves.

Chapter Fourteen

Caught-Up

2 Corinthians 12:1-4, "I must go on boasting. Although there is nothing to be gained, I will go on to visions and revelations from the Lord. (2) I know a man in Christ who fourteen years ago was caught up to the third heaven. Whether it was in the body or out of the body I do not know-God knows. (3) And I know that this man-whether in the body or apart from the body I do not know, but God knows- (4) was caught up to paradise. He heard inexpressible things, things that man is not permitted to tell."

When Paul says, "**I must go on boasting,**" he is referring to something he was addressing in the previous chapter. In verse one he says, "**I hope you will put up with a little of my foolishness.**" The "foolishness" he is referring to is his boasting of who he is and what he has done for God. Some false apostles, in fact he calls them super-apostles, had come along and were seeking to lead the Corinthian believers astray, so Paul has to re-establish his credibility with them by listing all of his accomplishments.

2 Corinthians 11:22-28, "Are they Hebrews? So am I. Are they Israelites? So am I. Are they Abraham's descendants? So am I. (23) Are they servants of Christ? (I am out of my mind to talk like this.) I am more. I have worked much harder, been in prison more frequently,

131

been flogged more severely, and been exposed to death again and again. (24) Five times I received from the Jews the forty lashes minus one. (25) Three times I was beaten with rods, once I was stoned, three times I was shipwrecked, I spent a night and a day in the open sea, (26) I have been constantly on the move. I have been in danger from rivers, in danger from bandits, in danger from my own countrymen, in danger from Gentiles; in danger in the city, in danger in the country, in danger at sea; and in danger from false brothers. (27) I have labored and toiled and have often gone without sleep; I have known hunger and thirst and have often gone without food; I have been cold and naked. (28) Besides everything else, I face daily the pressure of my concern for all the Churches."

It seems that by this point Paul says, *"I'm on a roll now. You got me started on this and I'm going to continue, so I must go on boasting."* However, right after this he says something quite interesting, *"There is nothing to be gained from all of this."* Paul was a spiritual man and he knew that boasting was emptiness and that it was only important to man. Men like to be puffed up, but this means nothing to God. Then he says, *"Look, if you really want to talk about something, let's go on to visions and revelations. I know a man that was caught up into the third heaven 14 years ago. He heard inexpressible things, things that man is not permitted to tell."* Most theologians believe that the "man" Paul was referring to was himself. That's also brought out later in the chapter when he talks about the surpassingly great revelations he had received from the Lord.

Further proof that Paul was not into boasting is the fact that this is the first account of this event. It happened 14 years prior and Paul had not shared it with anyone. That alone shows some credibility, because of the tendency for most of us to boast of our spiritual experiences. Men tend to believe that these kinds of experiences indicate they are "close to God." So without coming straight out and saying, *"You know I'm really close to God,"* we simply "share" about the great things we have done for God hoping people will make the connection. That lays the ground-work for what I really want us to focus in on in these verses. It's the fact that Paul was "caught-up."

When Paul said he knew a man who was "caught-up," he uses the Greek word *harpad'zo*. He was caught-up into paradise. It's from this word that we get the word or idea of "rapture." To be raptured or enraptured is to be caught-up or simply "taken-up." Perhaps you've heard of someone who was so "taken-up" with another person they couldn't think straight. That's what you call, "young love" (the inability to think straight). I heard once of a husband who said to his wife, "Honey, I love you terribly." She responded, "You certainly do."

The idea of the rapture comes from several scriptural references, but the one that is the closest to the idea of *harpad'zo* is:

1 Thess 4:16-18 "For the Lord himself will come down from heaven, with a loud command, with the voice of the archangel and with the trumpet call of God, and the dead in Christ will rise first. (17) After that, we who are still alive and are left will be caught up together with them in the clouds to meet the Lord in the air. And so we will be with the Lord forever. (18) Therefore encourage each other with these words."

The most popular perspective on this subject of being "caught-up" is the one that addresses a major end-time event when Jesus raptures His bride to be with him forever. However, don't you think it would be better to be in love before you are married? I have maintained for some time that the Church – the bride of Christ – is much more taken-up with her salvation than she is with her Savior. And there are significant hints in the scripture that you need to be caught-up with Him before you will be caught-up by Him. Some of this just makes common sense. How many men would want a bride that isn't that interested in them? How many would want a bride that is merely interested in your wealth, merely interested in getting married? In many ways that is how Christ's bride is today. We are not as "caught-up" with Him as we are with going to heaven.

I want to answer four questions: What does it mean to be "caught-up?" How do we become "caught-up?" Why is it important to be "caught-up?" What then happens to those who are "caught-up?"

1. What Does it mean to be "Caught-Up?"

I'm going to blend the two uses of this term to explain what it means to be "caught-up." Before you can be caught-up into paradise you need to be "caught-up" in your heart with the one you love.

Genesis 5:23-24 "Enoch walked with God; then he was no more, because God took him away."

To be "caught-up" means you no longer have an existence. This could be applied both figuratively and literally. If we are talking about the actual rapture of the Church, once you are raptured you no longer have an existence here on earth. If we are talking about a condition of the heart, the same could be said. In order to be "caught-up" in your heart with someone else, you no longer have an existence, because you have given them your heart.

We could look at this verse two ways. Enoch walked with God and God took him, subsequently, he was no more. Or we could look at it this way. The only way for Enoch to walk with God for over 300 years was because he was "caught-up" with Him. Therefore, because he was

135

"caught-up" with Him, he was "caught-up" by him. Enoch was not. Enoch gave up his existence in order to walk closely with his God. If we walk at a distance from him, it's because we are. We won't give up our existence. We love our life; we love our reputation; we love our status.

Paul was so concerned that he might take some glory from God by "boasting" of what he had done, that immediately after making the claims he says, in essence, but don't look at me. I have a thorn in my flesh that I cannot get rid of. I'm actually a weak man. He said, "I'm not even trained as well as the "super-apostles." Paul was not trying to gain a reputation as a "super-Christian." He was trying to direct his followers to the worship of Christ alone.

2. How do we become "caught-up?"

We must go after God! I think this is one of the most difficult issues we face in the Church today. How do we get people to want to be "caught-up?" Don't confuse this with the rapture of the Church. It would seem that all Christians want to be "caught-up" in the clouds with Him. The struggle is that of getting us to actually want Him now. Do you see what I mean by being more taken up with our salvation than our Savior? Everybody wants to go to heaven. Not everybody wants to walk intimately with Jesus today.

Enoch was "caught-up," because he walked with God for over 300 years.

During one Easter service I had my congregation come forward to attach a slip of paper on the cross. On that piece of paper they wrote down the various struggles they were having in their Spiritual life.

I was very saddened and surprised by how many people in my flock put down Spiritual lethargy as their problem. The word "lethargy" simply means "indifference." The problem with lethargy is that you don't care. You know you are not "caught-up" with Jesus, but you don't care. Lethargy also means sleepiness. In this case it would mean spiritual sleepiness.

Paul has a word for you:

Ephesians 5:14 "Wake up, O sleeper, rise from the dead, and Christ will shine on you."

There is a great truth in that. "Wake Up!" What do we think we are doing? We need to wake up! Why? Ephesians 5:16 tells us: "**because the days are evil.**" We live in very difficult days. Spiritually speaking, it is very difficult to live victoriously today.

Proverbs 2:1-11 "My son, if you accept my words and store up my commands within you, (2) turning your ear to wisdom and applying your heart to understanding, (3) and if you call out for insight and cry aloud for understanding, (4) and if you look for it as for silver and

search for it as for hidden treasure, (5) then you will understand the fear of the LORD and find the knowledge of God. (6) For the LORD gives wisdom, and from his mouth come knowledge and understanding. (7) He holds victory in store for the upright,he is a shield to those whose walk is blameless, (8) for he guards the course of the just and protects the way of his faithful ones. (9) Then you will understand what is right and just and fair--every good path. (10) For wisdom will enter your heart, and knowledge will be pleasant to your soul. (11) Discretion will protect you, and understanding will guard you."

Isn't that a great portion of scripture? Don't you want to understand the fear of the Lord and find the knowledge of God? If so, then you must search for it. You must store up the Word of God in your heart; you must turn your ear to wisdom; you must call out for insight and cry aloud for understanding.

In 1980, when I first began to give myself prayer, this was my favorite portion of scripture. I hung on to this in the prayer closet. I memorized large portions of God's Word. I would call out for insight while I was praying. Do you know what I found? Spending time memorizing God's Word is a key to insight into it. As you memorize something you must run it over and over in your mind. That's very similar to meditation. After a while, not only would I be able to recite the scriptures, they began to make sense to me. However, it didn't just happen. I had to go after it.

When Lou Ann and I were in Bible College, I found out that she was just crazy for me. At first I played hard to get – but then I remembered that I was actually easy - so I decided to let her catch me. She chased me until I caught her. I adjusted my work schedule to be with her. I offered to give her a ride to Church every Sunday. I went after her. Probably, most guys have their wives today because they went after them. You can't just sit around – you've got to show some interest. You've got to pursue. Now compare that to your pursuit of Jesus. Do you have any sense of putting extra effort into going after Him?

Proverbs says in essence, "If you would search for the things of God in the same way that you will search for gold – then you will understand the fear of the Lord and find the knowledge of God." Most men will put all kinds of time and effort into the pursuit of silver and gold, while they play with their commitment to God. Our jobs can make any demands on us that they want. But Jesus cannot get us to pray or read His Word consistently. You don't get "caught-up" by chance.

When we come to the parable of the ten virgins and how five of them were "caught-up" while five of them were not, we begin to see the significance of this. The five that were not "caught-up" were considered unwise. The wise were "caught-up." So Paul says in Ephesians 5:

Ephesians 5:15-16 "Wake up! Be very careful, then, how you live-not as unwise but as wise, (16) making the most of every opportunity, because the days are evil."

3. Why is it important to be "caught-up?"

This is easier to answer. Intimacy is the glue of a relationship. When you are "caught-up," you are bonded to Him. You come into a relationship with Him that has intimacy, secrecy, and power to it. After Paul admitted he was weak, he learned how to draw upon the grace of God. Three times he prayed for God to remove the thorn from his life. He wanted to be a strong man. Paul, like many of us, might have been tempted to live independently from God if he were strong, so God said, *"Paul, I want you close to me so I'm not going to make you a strong man; I'm going to make you a dependent man. Paul my grace can carry you through the difficult times. In fact, Paul, if you will learn to pray when you are weak, then my strength can be perfected in you because of your weakness."* Do you know how Paul responds to that?

2 Corinthians 12:10 "I delight in weaknesses, in insults, in hardships, in persecutions, in difficulties. For when I am weak, then I am strong."

Paul found that through being "caught-up" he drew so close to Jesus that no matter what happened to him he would

140

never leave Him. Paul never got over his weakness in this life. God did not even want him to.

4. What then happens to those who are "caught-up?"

Two things happen to those who are "caught-up" - humility and revelation. Paul's own admission of the "thorn" in his life must have been a humbling thing. It's not easy to tell your fellow man that you need something outside of yourself and that your own strength cannot handle a situation.

Micah 6:8 "And what does the LORD require of you? To act justly and to love mercy and to walk humbly with your God."

How can a man walk with God except with a humble Spirit? A proud man cannot walk with God because "He Is." Do you understand? Enoch walked with God because he was not. Only the humble man has the ability to be alive and, yet, not exist. The proud man cannot accomplish this. The proud man "is."

Walking with God is where revelation comes from. Revelation requires separation. Humility is a separation from the Spirit of this world. That separation opens you up to the Spirit world where revelation lives.

Paul said he received surpassingly great revelations from God. Paul lived a life set-apart from those around him. He was a completely sold out man, who was "caught-up" with his Lord. Subsequently, he was taken to the third

141

heaven and witnessed and heard things that are beyond man's comprehension. Paul's revelations and visions were so grand and wonderful that they were beyond description. Paul heard inexpressible things; things that man is not permitted to tell. Can you imagine what that would be like? Can you imagine how that would impact your life? How can a man receive from the Lord without being with the Lord? Vision and revelation are critical to our life. Without vision we perish, because we have nothing to live for. Before we can be caught up by Jesus, we must be caught up with Jesus.

Made in the USA
Middletown, DE
04 July 2017